MW00714792

Live Evil

A HOMAGE TO MILES DAVIS

Live Evil

A HOMAGE TO MILES DAVIS

RICHARD STEVENSON

THISTLEDOWN PRESS

© 2000, Richard Stevenson
All rights reserved

No part of this publication may be reproduced or transmitted in any form or by any
means, graphic, electronic or mechanical, including photocopying, recording, or any
information storage and retrieval system, without permission in writing from the
publisher. Requests for photocopying of any part of this book shall be directed in
writing to CanCopy, 6 Adelaide Street East, Suite 900, Toronto, Ontario, M5C 1H6.

Canadian Cataloguing in Publication Data
Stevenson, Richard, 1952–

Live evil: a homage to Miles Davis
Poems.
ISBN 1-894345-08-8
1. Davis, Miles—Poetry.   I. Title.
PS8587.T479 L48 2000   C811'.54   C00-920174-2
PR9199.3.S78728 L48 2000

Cover art by Marlene Ménard
Typeset by Thistledown Press Ltd.
Printed and bound in Canada

Thistledown Press Ltd.
633 Main Street
Saskatoon, Saskatchewan S7H 0J8
Canada
www.thistledown.sk.ca

  Canadian   Patrimoine
Heritage   canadien

Thistledown Press gratefully acknowledges the financial assistance of the Canada
Council for the Arts, the Saskatchewan Arts Board, and the Government of Canada
through the Book Publishing Industry Development Program for its publishing program.

ACKNOWLEDGEMENTS

This book wouldn't have been written were it not for the contributions of the following people:

Lyle Wesley, who first introduced me to Miles' music in the late sixties; Marlene Ménard, whose art and computer expertise led to the collaborative project, "Across Miles"; Sascha Feinstein and Yusef Komunyaka, whose excellent work, *The Jazz Poetry Anthology* (Indiana University Press, 1991) gave me a number of starting points; Quincy Troupe, whose biography, *Miles*, and poems, gave me a voice; Jack Chambers, whose definitive two-volume musical biography, *Milestones: The Music and Times of Miles Davis* (University of Toronto Press, 1983 and 1985) gave me further insights into the music and the man; Ian Carr, whose *Miles Davis: The Definitive Biography* (1998) and earlier edition (1982) helped as well; Joachime Berendt and Günther Huesmann, whose book, *The Jazz Book: From Ragtime to Fusion and Beyond*, clarified theoretical points and provided the necessary historical background; Daryl Long and Vanessa Holley, whose documentary comic books *Miles Davis For Beginners* (Writers & Readers Publishing, Inc., 1992) and *Jazz For Beginners* (Writers & Readers Publishing, Inc., 1995) helped me keep an overview; Richard Williams, whose coffee-table book, *The Man In The Green Shirt* (Bloomsbury Publishing Ltd., 1993) provided photos and crucial inspiration; Gary Carner, whose excellent festschrift anthology, *The Miles Davis Companion: Four Decades of Commentary*, gave me twelfth-hour inspiration; Anne Chambers, whose various anthologies, CD compilations, and critical works on the Beat Generation writers — male and female — provided a grounding in Beat poetics; Pearl Cleage, whose take on the domestic violence issues in *Mad At Miles: A Black Woman's Guide To Truth* (Michigan: The Cleage Group, 1990) revealed a side of Miles the biographies only touch on.

Thanks to the editors, producers, and curators of *The Antigonish Review*, *Arc*, *Backwater Review*, *Beatthief*, *Blue Buffalo*, *Blue Moon Review*, *Canadian Literature*, CBC's "Alberta Anthology", *Dandelion*, *Epistrophy: The Jazz Literature Archive*, *The Fiddlehead*, *The Gaspereau Review*, *Grain*, *It's Still Winter*, *Kairos*, *Kimera*, *The Kinté Space*, *The Lazy Writer*, *Lethbridge Living*, *Libel!*, *Losers First: Poems and Stories on Game and Sport* (Black Moss Press, 1999), *The Mississippi Review*, *Nebula*, *NetGuide Live* (Installation), *NeWest Review*, *paperplates*, *Prairie Journal of Canadian Literature*, *qwerte*, *Raw Nervz Haiku*, *Snakeskin: a Poetry Webzine*, *SEEDS*, *Textshop: a Collaborative Journal of Writing*, *Threshold: Anthology of Contemporary Writing in Alberta*, *Treeline*, *Urban Graffiti*, *The Wascana Review*, *WebLitCan*, *Whetstone*, *The Windsor Review*, *Ygdrasil*, and *Zygote* for accepting pieces from the working manuscript for publication, and to the Alberta Foundation for the Arts for a grant that helped keep the wolf from the door, and their patience in awaiting the arrival of the manuscript at theirs.

Finally, I'd like to thank my wife, Gepke, and my children, Adrian and Marika, for cutting me the necessary slack and putting up with the music, the discussions, the reading of rough drafts; the time they granted me definitely helped me put this one to bed.

CONTENTS

ALL UP IN MY BODY

THAT MOURNFUL BALLAD SOUND

HOOFIN' FOR HORSE

MILESTONES

KIND OF BLUE

BITCHES BREW

SILENCE

STAR PEOPLE

ALL UP
IN MY BODY

PANGAEA (1975)

ZIMBABWE

Two hundred million years ago
one super continent held all the
world's land mass in one funky stew
and to this principle, the world beat
fusion of funk, jazz, rock, blues,
you bend your horn and wail
cry out the pain of continents,
nations, countries being born; the pain
of cell division, of continents floating
on an impossibly hot liquid fire of magma
drifting apart and solidifying
just as the backbeat of bass and drums
lay down a foundation for the guitars
to shred their metallic notes all over
the psychedelic blues/fusion map
to fly like electrons away from the centre
but never quite fly out of orbit
and hold the most avant garde of blues/
free jazz in orbit around a simple rhythm
your horn scorching earth and everything
rolling in fat igneous currents
under you but never once losing your footing
until the notes slow down begin to jell
and your wah wah entreaty begins to sound
like the first creatures stirring
the first conglomeration of cells floating
volvox-like on the salt sea blues around you.

Your hip is killing you, your life is a mess.
You've pushed the limits of fusion and funk
way past psychedelia or anything Hendrix
might have done with you had he lived.

You've sorted and sieved all the sounds
and found free jazz wanting some structure,
pulled Buckmaster and Stockhausen into
the wild frenetic orbit of your techno blues
and kept the pure sound of your minimalist
cool horn floating — albeit shrieking like a raptor —
above all that land mass cooling, drifting
beyond your pain. Have somehow come up with
a hot live uncompromising blues sound that
is on the cutting edge of jazz without a falling
off the edge like Coltrane and Coleman before you.
Two lead guitars screaming ripping through
their solos shredding all the notes into
the most attenuated wails and primitive of cries
as though the sky itself were on fire.
Percussion, wah wah, bass funk lines
holding the whole simmering stew
in the cauldron before it boils over the top
and your one-hand organ vamps
put a lid on the volatile mix of styles.

1975, Osaka, Japan, the first of two concerts
a matinee and — this — the evening show —
the last you'd give before going into exile,
disassembling your horn, packing in
the musical odyssey to semi-retire
to a life of self-effacing chaos and abuse
as though you'd said it all in music and
now had to apply the theory of continental drift
to the various parts of your soul
teasing them out into separate island continents,
had to get down to magma
and watch its hot amoebic flow bud off
in phagocytic destructive fingerlings of pain

14

until you'd absorbed everyone and everything
in your social orbit into one hot pool
of bubbling red-hot terror
of formless, shifting pain.
And some of the critics could hate
the direction as much as you loathed
the self that disintegrated in the path
of that burning egoless lava flow
of elemental abuse. You'd burned down
the field and all the houses that stood
in the wake of everything you'd created,
quit because you "couldn't hear the music"
anymore. Only stood on the scorched earth
watching the smoking crust hardening into
scabs of rock, looking at the broken pillars
and debris of denuded tree trunks and
flaming branches, a forest of flames
ringing the whole pacific rim of truth.

So the first side of the disc trickles
down to a few bleats, blats, feedback shrieks
of Stockhausen-like electronic noise,
a few percolating notes of coffee-coloured percussion
that break through the crust like gas bubbles
in a mud flow, eventually becoming steam
and a calm wind jingling wind chimes
before the stinging applause of silence.

THE BLUE FLAME

For me fear is a little blue flame —
the first thing I remember
from my early childhood years,
a little blue flame jumping
from my Momma's gas range.

I don't remember lighting the stove,
but my head was very close
and the tiny spurt of fire
seemed to leap at me
like some snarling dog.

That fleeting blue flame
was sharp as a dog's tooth too
and I remember the heat —
jumping back, heart drumming;
being wide awake, and so afraid.

A little blue flame like a dog
straining the leash
snarling to get out of me.
Ever since, I've thrown that dog a bone.

Yeah. A skimpy blue flame.
That must be what fear of success
is too, I guess. And I just
turn up the gas, you know,
go a bit farther. Throw fear a bone.

I see that flame
clear as the music in my mind.
Always believed I needed to keep moving
to keep that flame from lickin' my heels.
Fame is a bitch too, you know.
A dog that's just whelped
has gotta protect its puppies

and a fine, sharp acetylene flame
has got to eat all the oxygen in a room.

They say most cats burn up
or burn out, that genius consumes
the soul or you become a match head.
Trane and Bird burned incandescent
for a time, and I might have too —

I felt the warmth then
come up over my spine
and lick at my insides like
I was just kindling on fire
every part of me collapsing into
a still centre where my soul
was nothing but a fragile
black match head.

I couldn't keep up with Diz at first,
then I didn't want to.
I'd seen Bird spiral like a moth
around the same pyrotechnic flame,
thought I'd cool out on my own tree.

THE VALUE OF MONEY

My father told me;
my grandfather told him,
Whenever you get money —
no matter where or who
you got it from, count it
to make sure it's all there.

You can't trust no one
when it comes to money —
fresh folding green is salad
to a goat. It just goes.
Relatives will nibble it
right out of your hand.

One time he gave my father a wad.
Said, "There is a thousand
dollars here. Go deposit it
in my account. But when my father
got to the bank, he came up short.
Counted only nine hundred and fifty.

He ran home with his heart
in his throat. Told grandfather
he'd lost fifty dollars.
My grandfather asked him,
"Did you count the money, son?
Do you know how much I gave you?"

He hadn't, of course, and didn't know.
Only then did Grandfather grin
and proffer the fifty in his fist.
The bank was thirty miles away;
it was a hundred in the shade
when my dad returned to deposit the rest.

"Trees don't put out fresh folding green.
And money don't provide shade
from the glare of the sun. Whitey
don't give the black man his due.
You'll be feeling the heat and sweat
a lot more than this before you are through,"

my grandfather said. And my father told me.
I count all my money now,
and hire lawyers to negotiate my fees.
What I feel through the soles of my shoes
flowers on the black stem of my horn.
Ain't no dumbass Davis ever born.

CLEANER THAN A BROKE DICK DOG

Before I got outta high school
I was giggin' all around St. Louis
playin' with Eddie Randle's Blue Devils —
or The Rhumboogie Orchestra
as the club owner preferred to call us.

I was makin' between sixty
and eighty-five dollars a week
and was cleaner than a broke dick dog
in my Brooks Bros. Suits and my Butcher shoes.
Boasted a brand new horn to boot.

Clark Terry customized that sucker for me too.
He was a wizard with the valves and springs
and taught me how to blow —
so did Fats Navarro — Fat Girl —
and Billy Danzig, best pickpocket I know.

I picked up some shit from a great
German trumpet teacher named Gustav
who played first trumpet with
the Symphony Orchestra in St. Louis.
He was a bad motherfucker too.

He also made great mouthpieces —
thin and deep — that gave me
that rich round sound. And I wanted
to be able to play like Harry James —
all of this before I met Diz.

I thought I was some shit hot trumpet player
in a city of shit hot players then,
But mostly I was shy and quiet
and put all of my words in my horn
like I wasn't some corn husker or rube

and the whole wide world
could be coiled like a hooker's fingers
that beckoned come hither
and compressed and detonated
in the three cylinders of my fine machine.

Oh yeah! I was clean, and cool,
was poised to pour pure ambrosia
into the ladies' ears. But don't ask me
why a dog's dick has gotta be broken
for a man's slacks to hang clean —

unless it's so the line, the crease
will hang sharp as a knife edge
and be unbroken clear to the hips
and give back the sheen of my
jutting jaunty hips without bunching.

We didn't want no manroot bulge
no gun-in-the-pocket or happy-to-see-you
tilts in our kilts. We wanted to float
you out of bed, out a window, round the block.

Jazz was hot, but we were cool
and you could cut thin slices
of the finest Gouda on the creases
of my trousers, honey. I was makin' money
for the first time in my life.

What I didn't know would fill buckets
like shucked peas. But this was St. Louis,
hog and cattle slaughter town.
My daddy was rich, fixed people's teeth
and Irene had the balls to get me this job.

She goaded me up that long, thin flight of stairs
and I auditioned for a seat in the band
I'd bragged was the "Only band in town."
Got a spot, much to my friends' chagrin.
I was sixteen and, man, I was clean.

I was happy. My heart beat stronger
than a sparrow flying headlong
into a window pane. The notes
didn't bead on my forehead either
for I was cleaner than a broke dick dog.

MEANWHILE, BACK AT THE RHUMBOOGIE . . .

I was walking past the dancers' dressing room,
and she called for me to come in, man.

I was all of seventeen and knew nothin', you know.
I mean, I was no virgin. Irene and me
we had a thing, but Dorothy Cherry?

She'd be twenty-three, twenty-four
and was finer than ten motherfuckers —
so fine guys'd send her roses every night.

Everyone wanted to fuck her. But I was stupid
about women then — except for Irene —
What did I know? She asked a favour; I obliged.

She asked me to hold a mirror under her pussy
while she shaved her pubic hairs, so I did.
I didn't think nothin' of it either, you know.

She was an exotic dancer; we played behind her show.
I just thought we were both entertainers.
It was show business, right? That's it.

It's not like I hadn't seen her gyrate
her fine low ass, hadn't seen those long legs, the way
she swung that long hair down her back before.

So I didn't think she had anything in store
for me that she doesn't put on display.
It was a job. It was how she earned her pay.

Anyway, the bell rang: end of intermission,
and it's time for the band to play again.
I told the drummer in the band what had happened.

The drummer'd be twenty-six or twenty-seven,
and he looked at me like I was some bull calf loon
and said, "So what did you do?"

I told him I just held the mirror for her
and he said, "That's all? That's all you did?"
and I said, "Yeah. What else was I supposed to do?"

"You mean with all the sex-fiend motherfuckers
in this band, she lets you hold the goddamn mirror?!"
he said. "Aw. Man, ain't that a bitch?!"

Then he started lookin' for someone else to tell,
and for a while the guys they start lookin' at me
like folks looked at my brother, Vern. Like I was gay.

Shit! That fine bitch havin' me hold that mirror,
and me lookin' at her sweet pussy —
She lookin' at me in that sly way women have —

Well, I graduated from high school that spring
and I got hip in a hurry, Jim.
Yeah . . . Dorothy Cherry — ain't that a bitch!

ALL UP IN YOUR BODY

The greatest feeling I ever had —
with my clothes on —
was when I first heard
Diz and Bird together.

I was up there, you know.
Bird was spirallin'.
Doin' shit no one had heard
in eight bars before.

I was hooked worse than
I would ever be on smack or C,
had to be where the music was,
had to be in New York City.

Had to have that sound
all up in my body then.
All the notes like black sedans
followin' too close in St. Louis.

So it was down to 52nd Street,
down to Harlem, down to Minton's,
all the way down to find
a cure for this monkey itch.

And you know there ain't no
script for this fever, Jim.
There was no name for
what these cats was puttin' down

but it was no uptown jive
and no one can say
what the motherfucker took to play
to drive away in each black note.

The traffic was fast
when Bird flew past
honkin' on his Cadillac.

Each high note Diz hit
had its top down, y'dig?
The notes they smelled of gasoline!

MINTON'S UNIVERSITY

We were all tryin' to get
our Masters degrees and PhDs
from Minton's University of Bebop
under the tutelage of Professors Bird and Diz.

It was a tougher school than Julliard
and what went down there took a while
to get to The Three Deuces, The Onyx,
The Downbeat and other clubs on The Street.

Bird was blowin' hard and fast
and only Diz could fly with him
and match those hot blues changes
in that upper register of his.

You had to be good to get on stage.
If you weren't and you got up
to play some sorry ass chords or fluffed
your solo or lagged behind the melody,

you'd not only get Fat Girl's
cold shoulders and wide ass to play to,
you'd get booed off the stage,
hauled out to the alley and beaten senseless.

You learned the black and blues, baby;
you didn't write no supplemental.
That was Bebop 101, and you were done —
back to the bush leagues in K.C.

Bird took his lumps in K.C. long before
he ever got to Harlem or 52nd Street.
Now here he was, a junkie motherfucker
noddin' in the suit he slept in —

until he put horn to lips and blew,
blew the doors off Bean, Jackie, Sonny —

all the ornithologists who watched him soar
or tried to ride the same dark horse.

But I didn't learn nothin' but confidence
from Bird. It was Bean — Coleman Hawkins —
who pushed me up on that stage.
He and Diz who showed me the changes.

And I changed, played the middle register
behind the beat while Bird took lead
and every night cried, "What do you need me for?"
while they just smiled. Then they came for me.

Feisty little Miles. Not yet twenty.
Shit! I couldn't grow a milk moustache!
Bean called me Sweet Cakes cos all I drank
was malted milks. I couldn't blow my nose!

Then Diz got sick of Bird missin' gigs,
noddin' off on stage, hockin' his horn
and only suit. Quit the baddest band
to ever play bebop. Made every jaw drop.

It wasn't just Chapter One that came to a close;
he closed the book on Bop, or so it seemed.
Then Bird decided he needed a different sound —
one that left him space to solo in —

and my spare, melancholy baby was born
of Lester and Lady Day: I leapt in
and set up the currents, the warm
thermals on which Bird soared.

That was Bebop 201. I passed!
Nodded in my daytime classes
until I finally got the nerve to tell Doc
I was droppin' out of Julliard.

DEXTER, ON SARTORIAL SPLENDOR

Dex came east in forty-eight
and we started hangin' out.
Played gigs and jammed 'n' shit.
He was real hip and dapper.

I thought I was super hip in my
three-piece Brooks Bros. Suits
(Niggers from St. Louis had a rep
for being sharp as a tack back then.)

But Dex, he set me straight
on the dress code thing. Said, "Jim
(Niggers was always "Jim" in them days)
Why don't you wear some other shit?"

"You can't be lookin' and dressin'
like that. You gotta get some vines.
You gotta go to F & M's, get you
some big-shoulder suits, Mr. B. shirts."

And I'd say, all hurt and shit,
"But, Dex, man, these some bad suits
I'm wearin'. I paid a lot of money
for this shit," thinkin' I was fine.

"Miles, man, that ain't it
cos the shit ain't hip.
See, style ain't got nothin' to do
with money. Style's an attitude.

I can't be seen with nobody
wearin' no square shit
like you be wearin', Jim.
We gotta change your attitude.

Man, you be playin' in Bird's band —
the hippest band in the world!

You oughta know better.
You ain't no parking validator!"

Now Dex, he's one of the hippest
and cleanest young cats
on the whole music scene,
so I'm listenin' to this jive.

He starts in on my physical self:
"Man, why don't you grow
a mustache or a beard?
Musicians gotta be cool. You too baby-faced."

"How, Dexter?" I say. "I ain't
got no hair growin' nowhere much
except my head and a little bit
under my arms and around my dick.

My family's got a lot of Indian blood
and niggers and Indians don't
grow beards and be hairy in their faces.
My chest is smooth as a tomato, Dex."

"Well, Jim, you gotta do something.
You can't be hangin' with us
lookin' like you're looking
cos you'll embarrass me," he says.

"Why don't you go get some hip vines
since you can't grow no hair?"
So I saved up forty-seven dollars
and got me a gray, big-shouldered suit.

After that trip to F & M's, Dex
came up to me grinnin' his big grin
towerin' over me 'n' shit,
and says, "Yeah, Jim, now you hip."

So I'm this kid in a big suit.
Got this shiny processed hair,
slicker 'n' goose shit and I'm
thinking I'm real cool.

Cool is a rule. And attitude
shows in everything I do now —
on or off the stage. But I dress
according to my own taste these days.

I set the pace. I'm miles ahead, see.
Gotta be. The paparazzis always be
poppin' off shots of me gettin' in
and out of my Lamborghini.

They like to see fine women
on a black man's arm. Can't be
tootin' no horn unless it's monogrammed
or black or red and shinier

than a motherfucker's bald head.
So I've always led — in fashion
and in music. It's how I keep
my dukes up. How I earned respect.

MONKEY SUITS

One time we're
playin' Birdland.
The manager tells us
we gotta wear uniforms.

All the cats did in those days,
but not Miles' band, man.
The next night Miles makes us
all stay in our dressing room
til it's time to take the stage.

Miles rolls a rack of clean threads
he got from a nearby men's wear
out on the stage and waits
til he has everyone's attention, eh.

"Oscar Goodstein wants to see
uniforms on stage," he says,
"so here they are. If you came
to gawk at uniforms and not
to hear the music, gawk away."

Then he leaves, cool as he arrived.
Everyone laughs for a while —
like Miles is up to some John Cage
trick or other, makin' better use
of silence than he usually does —

only the note turns sour,
hangs in the air like a bad fart —
not funky at all. And Oscar
he's lookin' at his watch,
sweatin' like ol' Satchmo.

He's got no hanky, see.
The hubbub is startin' to look mean.

Goodstein backs down on his demand
and then we take the stand
to grand applause. Miles gives Oscar a wink.

It weren't no big thing, and Oscar he
doesn't say a word, just nods.
Miles blows a long, lean note
and leans back on his haunches.
We bring down the moon with the house.

BIRTH OF THE COOL

It's not like you fired a salvo
from The Royal Roost
or burned down Minton's
with a fiery wad of some
low tech f/x cannon.

"Move" and "Jeru" bop along
with reduced big band moxie,
but are orthodox enough boplicity;
the meter's fast, the lines rhyme,
so to speak: very Swing Street.

Very forties too, if less urgent,
less frenetic than bebop. This then
playing jazz tennis without the net?
Your reduced orchestral palette
so sweet to head and feet

marched smartly off to the West Coast
tout de suite. Discreet is the word
for that invasion. Subtle. Fleet.
Your horn so sweet and clean —
almost an amalgam of bop and swing —

a new thing that has my toes tappin'
to what I'm mapping now
as I turn the corner of this line
or the next. A nest to rest on.
The pigeons coo and thrum,

beating at my clavicles from
atop a warm drumlin
of the heart. Not a high perch, no.
Not a peak ascended breathless,
without compass or maps —

certainly nothing you need
pure oxygen to breathe to survive.
But, oh, how the traffic slows down
as first one note and then the next
fills out the checkerboard

on the doors of the cars that carry me:
Piet Mondrian's Boogie Woogie
become a cab insignia? Assured
as a skink slinking in and out
of traffic. So cool! So fleet! So sleek!

THAT
MOURNFUL
BALLAD
SOUND

JULIETTE GRECO

April '49: Tadd and I
take a band to Paris
to play opposite Bird.

It's my first gig overseas,
away from The Street.
I love Paris; Paris loves me.

Tadd, Klook, Moody,
Michelot and I
swing hard and bop.

Pierre lays down
a fat, funky bass stew;
Klook simmers cymbals into cool.

I ride, light and airy
over the top,
parachute glissandos

down the middle
and in the groove,
bob and weave —

I'm Sugar Ray.
I'm a butterfly on rock.
I've got Paris in my pocket.

I fete with Picasso,
Sartre and du Beauvoir,
eat crepes and croquettes.

A beautiful woman
glides into the room,
self-assured, full of grace.

Her face is exquisite,
her hair long and black.
I know I have to meet her

and I do. She is Juliette.
We go to the Louvre,
walk hand-in-hand along the Seine.

I have no French; she has no English.
Each touch becomes a language
we learn to read in Braille.

I want to sound her every note,
pluck her every string
against the fretwork of her spine.

She wants me to stay.
I don't want to leave.
Irene and the children call.

It's a deep blue groove;
for the first time in my life
I'm hanging on every note.

My horn is hatless,
could blow down walls,
every note, a petal,

falls.

HEROIN

It's a level of consciousness,
a fundamental fact,
a lover, a language,
a passport of flesh.

A pilot light in the soul
leaps up in that little blue flame
to kindle all the synapses
in the old lizard brain.

The body's paraffin melts,
rises up the wick
while the new molecule
makes truth one candle only.

A cognitive wind
blows over the soul,
words' brittle stalks
quickly catch fire.

It is that point —
the point of combustion
when all language ignites,
when all words become one word,

when all emotions
become one emotion
that matter becomes
insubstantial, so immaterial.

What is the set point of desire?
Why, when the curtains are burning,
do we most desire
to walk through the flames?

At the corner of Knowledge
and Public Edifice
the shadowman stands
whistling "Parker's Mood".

All around him the city burns,
pieces of the sky keep falling,
already a tiny blue flame
is licking up his veins.

In minutes or perhaps hours
another man will appear.
Neither will notice
the other's hair burning.

"HEY, MATINEE!"

"Hey, Matinee! Whatchew doin' man?"
"Not much — and you?"
"Runnin' with my main man Jackie.

"Bin up to Manhattan every day
to see the man, hang with Sonny
and jam, keep my chops up.

But I ain't bin giggin' in months,
haven't cut no wax in a year,
don't get home enough, you know . . . "

So he looks at me like I'm nuts
'n' says, "You got a habit, nigger?
You better come with me."

He buys me smack in Queens.
First time I scored in the 'hood
and my nose is runnin' and shit.

Nervous as some one-eyed
bedraggled cat in an alley.
I hadn't cranked. Hated needles.

But I was a sorry-assed mo' fugger.
Didn't know! Didn't believe!
I was too hip to be hooked!

I snorted the stuff.
Kept snortin' 'til next time
Matinee sees me, says, "Miles,

This ain't nose candy, boy.
You're sick. You've graduated
to the needle now."

I wanted to get off the stuff
from the first time I spiked,
but I had to stay cool to play.

I started runnin' a stable of whores.
Even chose my jobs
in places I could score.

Lost my chops.
Lost gigs and record deals.
Lost the Downbeat poll.

I was a former All-Star,
Has-been Re-bopper,
One-time Blue Devil.

But I wanted to bed
this bitch called fame,
ride her til I was old and lame.

Nothing I spiked or snorted
carried the whack on the head
of that blue flame.

I had miles of aisles to fill,
I had a hunger and a will.
I had a hunger and a will . . .

THAT MOURNFUL BALLAD SOUND

1. "Baby Won't You Please Come Home"

First Victor tickles the trickle
of rainwater from the eaves
then comes that mournful
harmon mute and I'm
clean as mist evaporating
from the leaves of grass
before my foot falls anywhere
on this pristine lawn and I
know my baby's gone for good
this time and though that muted
horn sounds like a begging fool
I know the admission of failure
in these notes is just another
cool rebuke and the sadness
is the sadness of the bell of a flower
heavy with its drink and no hurt
can slake the thirst like that
first cool drink of memory.

2. "Once Upon a Summertime"

Once upon a summertime it was
before there was the ache of success
or the need to drink from sad Elysian streams.
Once upon a summertime when there were horses
high upon a ridge top and cattle lowing,
the only mournful creatures on the farm;
once upon a summertime when the raindrops
were prisms of the heart and broke the world
into colours no one knew the names of
and there were rabbits — dozens — on the lawn
and I picked up that trumpet of fate
and eased those doeskin notes out of the bell

and they tumbled and slurred and fumbled
for the labial folds of the rose with such an ache;
once upon a summertime before Irene
teen pregnancy and even newspapers delivered
door to door there was no floor or ceiling
to the notes and I bent them with such
dexterity once upon a summertime upon a time
there was summer and all the leaves
and the birds and the bees were singing to themselves.

3. "I Fall In Love Too Easily"

Sometimes a sweet orchestral sound
was what it took to fall in love
but I fell in love so easily, so completely,
I played with that sweet, clean sound.
And I was no Diz no Satchmo no Harry James
out on a strut and no fool hangin' from a tree
but I fell in love too hard and too easily
and my muse was sweet and fickle
tasted so like treacle or ice water to the teeth
and I put all my words — selected carefully —
like long stem roses into the beautiful vase
of that gold bell and I fell in love too easily
and George Coleman called me long distance
on the tenor saxophone and talked patiently
and in such soft comforting tones and spoke of
rambles and ambling free while Frank Butler
laid down the pitter patter bash thump
of what he carried in his trunk in the Seven
Steps he took to Heaven and he said
you fall in love too easily ride the wind
like the first lie on a gentle breeze
and we all fall in love too easily.

4. "Song # 2"

The mute is off but the tune is soft
and I mean to confide something new
through the carefully chosen few
notes I set before you like a glass of claret.
Something about the second love of my life
and how the first would always leave a thirst
for more than any orchestra could give
with me hanging so alone out there on a note.

How the mute gave me a soft low corner
of my self to explore in those early
mourning hours. How it says Song # 1:
the first time is never done and how
stolen apples are so sweet from the tree
or how singing can make me free, free to
abandon the tune in my every muscle
in my every cell and fibre of being
saying I'm ready always ready
for Song # 3. And Song # 1 is never done.

5. "Bye Bye Blackbird"

Up tempo now and swinging atop the tree
of improvisational zeal, no one else has
my feel for this classic piece. A breeze
whistles through the branches, riffles the leaves
and I take the melody where I please.
Who could ever imagine dying of complications
of pneumonia and a stroke when each walking
bass line throbs with the full-blood thrust
of intent and invention? Such delicacy! Such strength!
The blackbird himself sits atop a bulrush
bobbing with the breeze. Its feet cling to the promise

of rebirth in each compacted seed the way I
hold each compacted note with such assured
breath and grace. Right now death is years away,
not even a bleeding on the horizon. I am riding
midday like a kid at the midway. So self-assured.
Wynton Kelly's piano notes feel like bare feet
on steaming compacted mud. There is a child
parting the rushes, his ear cocked to hear the
redwing's beautiful song as it bobs and Hank
Mobley's got such a sweet sound he might
be holding the moment for me to peer through
those rushes with my horn. No rebuke, no scorn . . .
Jimmy Cobb holds the rhythm that keeps such innocence
still and rides the cymbal so the bird can trill.
Bye Bye Blackbird, I want to sing. I'll take
it all. Take it all on the wing and glide with you
note for note, stalk to stalk. This is how we
both train our voices to arch in the wind.

6. "Wait Till You See Her"

Wait till you see her. My muse is so
lovely in her bones, is a dancer who floats.
Wait till you see her. You won't believe
the ache her hesitancy inspires. The fire
in the loins, the heart to see her part
her hair. Wait till you see, She is
every note I could hope to play. Every
note I'd ever want to hold out to love,
the whole bouquet. Wait till you see her,
then you'll really hear me play! I'll stay
the crease in every rose and give you such
a whiff of grace in every permutation and fold.
Wait till you see her ghostly presence glide

47

down from the blue halo of smoke
in this room. She holds the air like a balustrade.
An ingenue of impossible beauty and grace.
Wait till I make her appear and disappear.
You will never fear your loneliness again.

7. "Basin Street Blues"

Basin Street is the street
where the elite always meet
in New Orleans
my land of dreams . . .

Where are we going? Does anyone know?
The road to Mississippi is long and
New Orleans is crowded with dead horn players
trying to find a way home. Does anyone know
the way up from the streets where the rich
sit sipping gin? Does anyone know how really
mournful this ballad business is? Slowing
down the tempo to find the way out of the old
to the unexpressed emotion? Where are you, Louis?
I use a mute and play these blues slowly
so I can hear each and every note and know
what it means — this cry — this sad, hollow
reach from the belly of hunger to the bright
ravening reach of the stars. I had a dream
and Kansas City was its name. I had a shot,
a reach for fortune and fame. I ache and I ache
for a place to call my own. I hang on each note
like a child in a tree swinging on an old tired tire.

8. "Corcovado"

Jobim, I'm sorry. Your "Corcovado",
your bossa nova notes move like a
slow river in my soul. I am
listless and even your lovely melody can't
save *Quiet Nights* from bathos today.
I want the engineers to stop this madness,
to put it in the can, save it for a rainy day.
I told Teo I can't have anything more
to do with this recording. Gil is patient
but composes and arranges too slowly.
I've lost my conviction. Can you hear me, Jobim?
The notes have found bottom. I pole my way
along this slow-moving river and suddenly
know the pull of gravity. How the years
accumulate a sediment of old sentiments
and news, how the muck and ooze suck
at a man's marrow, and I know the blues.
Stan Getz has beat me to the punch by two months.
His first bossa nova kicks ass.
I should have understood. The critics will
pronounce this record sludge. It's just this side
of late night, cocktail stasis. I hate it.
I tried to float the notes up in the canopy
where I saw you just now, your splendid
shimmering grace a flash of red and green —
the fabled quetzal giving back its incandescence
to the corner of my eye, but you flew out of range.
Jobim, the current takes me. I'm quite overcome.
Tell me what it means when each note is a feather
falling. How to calculate the height of the trees
from two separate points in our two hearts.
I cannot find the azimuth of desire and all
around me the trees are burning. The trees are burning.

HOOFIN'
FOR HORSE

R.I.P.

Folks here funky in their bones —
They don't sell policies or plots;
they got no garden gnomes.

ON THE ROAD (1952)

Dope in the Midwest was scarce
Jimmy and I had a hard time scorin'.
We were late gettin' to gigs.
The band would start before us —
at intermission too
we'd be cruisin' for drugs.

These weren't concert gigs either.
They were more like dances.
A cat called Symphony Sid played MC.
That's all the motherfucker did,
and he got paid three times
what they paid all of us!

We'd find or be found by
some dealer in the audience.
Go back to the hotel to crank
and get down. Be late gettin' back.
The guys'd get nervous or pissed,
rag on us to get our act together.

Percy'd be all up in his brother's face,
and then he and Milt and Kenny
would be shittin' all over me.
Relations between Sid and the band
got out of hand too. He'd not show
and we'd split his purse.
Things went from bad to worse.

We'd get five hundred bucks —
eighty-three and change apiece;
he'd pocket two grand,
tell us his take was seven C's —
Bags overheard the prick
talkin' turkey with the club owner

that time. Sonnuvabitch was
gettin' ten percent of the gate
and announcer pay too!

We'd bitch and he'd say
we were ungrateful!
Now ain't that the white way!
We got back to New York
and didn't want to see
the motherfucker after that.

He owed J.J. fifty bucks
and fluffed him off for it
(Sid was an arrogant motherfucker),
so J.J. up and knocked
Sid's false teeth out of his mouth.
They went skippin' 'n' skiddin'
clean across the floor.

Then Sid called in these gangsters
who came down to the club.
They were gonna kick J.J.'s ass,
looked cartoonish and natty
in their black suits and hats,
suckin' on stogies, makin' a show
of takin' off their coats.

One of 'em asked me if I
was with J.J. I told him I'd stand
behind his motherfuckin' ass.
The rest of the band gathered round
and we squinted at each other
through Bogie clouds of blue smoke.

It was Sid who chilled us out.
He finally paid J.J. what he owed,
but that was some shit
we had to go through. My jones
was climbin' my spine, swingin'
like a jesus monkey from a lamp post,
tin cup in hand. I'd a gone
to the grave for that band!

VOLUME ONE (BLUE NOTE)

All the takes from Alfred Lion's
Blue Note sessions one and three
in the order they were recorded,
plus an alternate take of "Chance It",

and, suddenly, thanks to the miracle
of modern day digital transfer, here you are
unspooling your May to June romance
like a hula hoop around the moon.

"Dear Old Stockholm", "Donna", "Yesterdays",
"How Deep Is The Ocean", and other ballads
suddenly rustling like crinoline or
a zephyr disturbing "Autumn Leaves" —

Selections 1-9 recorded May 9, 1952
at WOR Studios, New York City;
Selections 10-15 recorded March 6, 1954
at the Van Gelder Studios, Hackensack, New Jersey . . .

Such painstaking restoration. One thinks
of a home transformed into an objet d'art
of Frank Lloyd Wright's "Falling Water"
with its year-round caretakers, or the face lifts

necessary to keep the Sphinx in the pink.
It gives you pause to think there is
no nose missing. No Mona Lisa smile
to extricate from wrinkle lines of old paint.

The music is fresh, not hermetically sealed
like a can of Columbia-grown coffee.
The "soaring spurts of lyrical exultancy
outnumbered by somber moments of pensive gloom,"

according to Leonard Feather, who has so lovingly
dusted off his copies of the original LPs.
But, really, these are spring leaves sprouting
from nearly dead limbs. The xylem and phloem

don't carry water and nutrients from
some deep aquifer of emotion so much
as a mix of hope and addiction that
flowers in the poppies of your lacklustre eyes.

You are playing from the other side of longing.
The eggshells you walk on belong to hatchlings
that have fallen from the nest, not angels.
Your muse is a cuckoo, a hard-bitten bitch

with her own mouths to feed. Every time
you lift your arms to the sun to play,
their Edward G. Robinson mouths gape
from your pores. Their eyes look like roof nails.

These were two chances. Your life a series
of alternate takes. You play like the child
who would climb out on the highest limb
to see if there are any eggs left in the nest.

KICKIN' H

I tried to kick; hell, every addict does.
Bird tried tankin' up on vodka;
Red got sent up to the Big House —
had no choice but to trade
one steel cage for another.

Most don't make it; many get off
and on like it's some kind of
ghetto trolley and they
gotta get to the end of the line
to see their pie-in-the-sky.

I had to go to Millstadt —
to the prize pigs and cows
of my Daddy's farm. Ride
my big stallion H like some
bone-rack jockey in a Steeplechase.

A week locked up in a room
with my family playin' nursemaids
finally bucked me from my pride,
though I was an absentee landlord,
the castle of my skin some slum tenement

for years after that. Ain't your jones
who holds the keys. It's the
feral cat lookin' back from the mirror
with sharp shards in its green eyes
that has learned to take what it needs.

I puked myself inside out
until I could smell the grass again,
walked and talked and emptied
my self like a goddamn bucket.
Even had a girlfriend drain my spuds.

I knew I'd have to mainline music
if I was gonna stay away from this
subtle muse. She's the womb of wombs,
and lots would choose to write graffiti
on her walls rather than fall foal-like

into the green arms of this world.
Even the damn sunlight hurt!
Every nerve stuck me like a needle.
My skin bristled. If I could
make music do this, I could grow quills!

MILESTONES

BAKER'S KEYBOARD LOUNGE

For five years you've prowled the streets
like Rilke's panther behind bars of rain,
taken Bob Weinstock's shitty pay to cop,
record lacklustre tunes in a desultory mood.

You've fluffed solos, lost your pride
and embouchure, slid with the grains
of sand in your hourglass veins,
convinced you were living on borrowed time.

Fat Girl's dead; Bird's flame gutters
on fifty-second street; the wax flesh
of zombie boppers everywhere melting,
unable to resolve itself into a dew.

The brownstones are covered in a soot
from Europe's chimneys. The homeboys
all want stand-up and burlesque,
the music is now a watered drink.

So you slink along the streets of Detroit
from your low-paying gig at the Bluebird
to Baker's, try to insinuate your self
between the heavy drops of rain and sweat.

Rain on your face and in your hair,
your clothing and demeanor soaked,
the driest thing about you your trumpet
cradled like a baby under your coat,

you weave your way through the crowd,
up to the bandstand when Clifford blows
"Sweet Georgia Brown" and Max Roach
and Ritchie, Bud Powell's little brother, keep time.

Oblivious to the group, the people, the place,
parked in the big bend of the baby grand,
you put your trumpet to your lips,
launch into "My Funny Valentine".

Brownie stops blowing, cues the boys
to prop you up, while the audience
gathers like iron filings from
off the corner, around the block.

And the water courses down your cheeks
as, in the midst of your defeat, you
wail to the elements: Love me, love me
just a little, let the rain wash me clean.

It's a sad performance; you're bad.
Every time you push a valve
is like spiking a needle in your arm
and pushing the plunger home.

The last note haunts you, follows you,
a black sedan you hadn't noticed before.
Soon the driver will pull over to the curb
and beckon you to get in.

MILES' TAKE ON SUGAR RAY

Boxing's a science, man.
I watch it whenever I can.

Consider, for instance,
the art of the jab.

When a cat slips the jab
you gotta know his habits.

Will he deke left or right?
It ain't about mass or might.

The speed with which he dekes
is matter in motion, you see.

You double the velocity of impact
if your other fist can meet a cat's conk.

You gotta have style in whatever you do —
writing, music, painting, fashion . . .

A boxer is a dancer on speed.
Sugar Ray's got everything he'll ever need.

He knows when to fake,
when to bob and weave.

He'll smack a guy three
times upside his head

then switch to his side,
then go back to his head.

A cat gets ornery
when he's cornered or caught.

Ray's got the rhythm,
his jabs are like jazz.

Always in the pocket.
It takes a knack to know.

You don't get it by guess or by golly.
You gotta know, gotta be shown.

The man's fists are the valves
of the trumpet he plays.

I've learned as much about time
and where to float the notes

from watching Sugar Ray dance
as I ever learned from playin' with cats

on any music stand. That's a fact.
Ray's like Bird, a genius in my corner.

It was watchin' him box got me
to kick my habit. He laughs when I say so

but he knows: it takes more than jive talk
for a man to k.o. his jones.

A man can't dance
with a monkey on his back.

I had to know my jones
to knock him to the mat.

JULIETTE COMES TO NEW YORK

Summer 1954:
I got no jones
doggin' my bones,

have done "Walkin' ",
found a new
funky urban blues.

Juliette calls
and my heart
won't stop jumpin'.

They want her
for the screening of
Hemingway's novel.

I want her so badly too
I don't know what to do
with my new emotions.

You'd think
the sun had risen
on my black ass,

but I'm too stunned,
too afraid
to make a pass.

She calls me
and what do I do?
Bring a drummer —

as if I need
Art Taylor
to keep time for me.

She's crestfallen, confused
and all I can do
is refuse and abuse.

I say, "Juliette,
give me some money!
I need money right now!"

I want to fall
into her ready arms,
make passionate love.

Instead, I look at her
as if she were
something to eat.

She wants to know
if I can come to Spain.
I say I'll call.

The truth is
I'm haunted by ghosts,
don't know friend from foe.

My jones
won't let anyone in
the castle of my skin.

He's an absentee landlord,
still owns my soul.
I have miles to go.

BLUES FOR BIRD

Shit, Bird! What am I
supposed to do with this
bogus news? You know I ain't
no rube in piped pajamas
about to make a steeple of my hands
now that they've lain you down to sleep.

Yeah, I got red silk pajamas —
right now I'm a quetzal in a cage,
if you want to know the truth.
Irene, she made me for a piker
on the child support, so here I sit
on Riker's Island, pissed past purple.

I'm not gonna piss and moan
or whistle "Parker's Mood" for you!
You were always a glutton, there was never
any hourglass big enough to squeeze
all these white sand grains through.

I'm not nineteen any more —
I'm way past the malted milk moustache;
I got tired of the sweet stuff too.
Do you have any idea how many fools use
just so they can pretend to soar with you?

You left a hole bigger than the one
where all the money went, Yard.
Now the junkies are keepin' junk time;
no fix can save their souls.
The dragon is teachin' end rhyme
and the sad fact that eyes are holes.

Birdland is no aviary!
All the ornithologists you wooed
are sloppy seconds compared to you!

The cage of your ribs couldn't hold
the damaged red bird forever, man.

You know. Even if the coroner,
looking at your lovely plash of organs,
had you pegged for sixty-five,
the ugly print runnelling down the page
will scream thirty-four! thirty-four!

What for, man? Because you
couldn't find a cheaper script
than the one on the street? "Bird lives!"
the graffiti weeps on tenement walls.
"Bird lives!" Why should I weep for you?

You said it yourself back in fifty-three.
Remember? You called me Lily Pons
and intoned in a sorry ass British accent,
"To produce beauty we must suffer pain —
from the oyster comes the pearl."

"Man, fuck you and the horse you
rode in on," I wanted to say,
but I just sputtered and spit
my way through the take that day
cos you and I go back a long way.

Yeah, I'll miss you, Bird,
but you still piss me off.
I can't forget the time in a cab
that bitch gobbled your cock
while you sat beside me.

You had your greasy mouth
around a drumstick and just grinned
while I hung my head out the window

like some ear-flappin', nose-twitchin' dog.
Elmer Dumbfuck in back of the truck.

That ain't me no more, and the truth is
that I kept those early sessions on track.
You were too fucked up, Bird!
Now you're fuckin' me up again!
I loved you, you dumb shit!

1955, NEWPORT JAZZ FESTIVAL

We played "Now's The Time" for Bird,
then got down on Monk's "Round Midnight".
I played it with a Harmon mute.
The crowd went crazy. I got a long ovation.

When I stepped down from that stage
people looked at me like history was made.
I was a king; they were ready to pay homage.
The suits started offering record deals.

It was somethin' else, but, man,
I'd mastered that tune an age ago,
had laid down fatter tracks on wax.
Why was I so shit hot now?

Not that I was grumblin' y'understand.
I took my bow and you better believe
I loved puttin' those other cats in the shade,
so, sure, I ate the little sandwiches,

did a turn or two on the broadloom,
so to speak, til Elaine came over
with these grinnin' silly white folks
who wanted to meet the badass player.

"Oh, this is the boy who played
so beautifully. What's your name?"
the silly bitch says, smiling away
like she's done me some favour.

"Fuck you. I ain't no fuckin' boy.
My name is Miles Davis.
You better remember that
if you ever want to talk to me," I snapped.

I got Monk and Harold and split.
To hell with that black boy
crossin' knees and sippin' gin
on the Heppelwhite shit. I don't do that gig.

ASCENSEUR POUR L'ECHAFAUD
(Lift To The Scaffold)

It is nineteen fifty-seven.
You are the enfant terrible
from St. Louis, a not-yet-famous
jazz trumpet player. The three-week
tour of Europe is not a bust, but
still, only consists of five dates.

You have time on your hands.
Marcel introduces you to the head
of his production crew. He is doing
work on a black and white film —
Louis Malle's first foray into features
after scuba pics with Jacques Cousteau.

Everything is still underwater strange.
Jeanne Moreau cannot rescue the plot,
won't play the female lead in The Lover
for another year. Right now she has
a husband to kill and the perfect crime
in a not-so-hot film noir to botch.

Louis Malle shows you some rushes.
You agree to do the soundtrack —
it seems an interesting project. Why not?
The French musicians have been touring
with you. Louis will provide the film
loops he wants you to score.

It's a matter of noodling at the keyboard
of a piano in your hotel room,
getting a feel for Parisian rain
and fog. Walking the Champs Elysees
at night, insinuating yourself between
the shadows of the grainy images you see.

But the hours you spent insinuating
the thin blade of your shoulders between frames
will cast a shadow even you could not anticipate.
That tone, so ethereal, so haunting —
especially with the echo chamber effects
in Louis' out-takes, will dog your steps forever.

The distance between notes is the distance
the accused travels in each step to the scaffold.
Dem be some badass blues. Cool as the slab,
haunting as the last heartbeats, the crack of the neck.
Each note is a crow. The score hunkers in staves
that make every image, every still, a grave.

MILESTONES (1958)

After all the junk and lacklustre playin',
after Walkin', Workin', Cookin', Steamin',
Relaxin' with you; after Newport
(your sweet Harmon mute), your Columbia debut,
where could you possibly take us to?
What mode of transport would you choose?

You've taken us way past midnight
on the big hard bop clock. Why not
Flyin', Cruisin', Blisterin', Bruisin', Fusin'?
You've certainly gained speed and altitude.
"Dr. Jeckyll's" test tube is full of jet fuel.
Why not fly straight with no chaser?

When you're breathin' in the stratosphere
what fear could tether you to terra firma?
The only place left to look is down —
down to the low rumble of the guts,
the smolderin' furnace of the blues. You fuse
everything into fuel rods with this sextet.

Implode even as you explode convention
playin' time and changes. And what a red-hot
reactor you've got! Cannonball and Trane?
Philly Joe, Red Garland, and Paul Chambers?!
No wonder you look so cool in your green shirt,
sleeves rolled up, brow furrowed in a quizzical look.

You hold your trumpet like a simple offering,
as if to say, "What, this? I just turn lead
to gold in these three chambers here. Excuse me
while I empty my li'l brass horn of ambrosia
and spit." As if it were that simple to blister
all the paint off walls. Man, you don't let it dry!

'58 SESSIONS

So sweet on "On Green Dolphin Street",
"Fran Dance", and "Stella By Starlight"
with Bill Evans in your corner. No one —
not even that funny valentine, Chet Baker,
with his ravaged schoolboy / James Dean looks,
could touch you and your Harmon mute on ballads.
'58 must have been some Doris Day dream
you never woke from. All the hedges clipped like poodles
and Howdy Doody freckled chicklet-toothed rubes
smiling from every cornflakes box. Gosh! Could
it be the big ones Truman dropped really were
mushrooms and we all nibbled at their spore-filled
caps like beady-eyed mice? Was everything really
so terribly nice? The blue tinge of longing
you gild the roses with suggests not. But still,
so much of life fit into these beautiful bars.
Who would have thought that all that space foreplay
that would put man in the moon's labia would be preceded
by your forays to the farther planets, Venus and Mars?

You had "Love For Sale", wanted life
straight with no chaser. Could cleave
atoms on the clean creases of your pants.
No ants in 'em. At least not up there on stage.
You were the quintessence of cool in those days.
Our Funny Valentine taking all the oil
out of Rollin's Oleomargarine and compressing
it to such a pure golden yellow substitute
for butter we all took to having toast and
two eggs, sunny side up, for breakfast.

Cannonball and Trane took your box cars
around so many turns of track loneliness
had a new name. We called it Miles
after distance covered; you made it feel
like home though we could never go there again.

74

"YOU'RE UNDER ARREST!"

Being rebellious and black,
cool and hip, sophisticated;
being clean, a nonconformist,
playin' the fuck outta my horn
earned me nothing but scorn
and derision in some quarters —

but it was an image that played
to the hip fifties generation,
and muggin' and grinnin'
like Pops or Diz was no way
for a black artist to behave
in those heady blue smoke days.

I was no Uncle Tom nigger
and Marlon Brando and James Dean
were all the rage, had set
the pace for that in-your-face
Rebel-Without-a-Cause, brooding,
moody, existential hero thang.

They wanted niggers with attitude —
on the stage. And I gave 'em
cool, brooding, introspective in spades,
but there was no way a good ol' boy
pounding rain-slicked pavement
was gonna tolerate a cool black blade.

I had just done an Armed Forces Day gig —
a Voice of America broadcast
for our men in khaki. Was tired
of that red, white, and blue crap.
A beautiful white woman named Judy
needed a cab, so I hailed her one.

"Move along, son," this white cop says
like I'm some no count nigger
hopped up or jiggin' for change.
So I point up to my name
on the marquee, say, "That's me,
Miles Davis. I'm just gettin' some air."

Motherfucker grins and goes into his bag,
"I don't care where you work.
I said, 'Move on!' If you refuse,
I'm going to arrest you." Just like that.
And, of course, he gets more pissed,
so I look at his face straight and hard.

I don't move. I ain't gonna take
no stain from this jiveass motherfucker.
So he says, "OK. You're under arrest,"
and steps back. Being a boxer, I think
the sonnuvabitch is gettin' ready
to crack me one on the cranium.

I step closer, so he'll have no reach.
The motherfucker trips and tumbles
before he can unhitch his cuffs.
Then out of the inevitable clutch
of rubberneckers suddenly there comes
this billyclub. BAM! Right on the nut.

Some other jiveass buffoon
is now callin' the tune and I'm off
in a paddy wagon to the local constabulary
before you can say Sugar Ray Robinson.
Blood is runnin' down my khaki suit
and — goddamn! — there's nothin' I can do!

Fuckers charged me with resistin' arrest!
Charge might have stuck too if I
didn't have Harry Lovett in my corner.
As things stood, the story — and charge —
made the front pages of the New York papers.
Frances came down and threw a fuckin' fit.

Maybe it was the sight of a beautiful
light-skinned woman wailin' over
my kiwi black ass got the cops thinkin'
they might have fucked up. But, sure enough,
it took three judges two friggin' months
to clear me of that sillyass charge.

It was the sight of a handsome black buck
on the arm of a gorgeous white woman
that fucked up the pig who'd obstructed me.
And that changed how I thought about race.
The buggers ended up eating crow, but,
even so, they had my cab card revoked.

That's why I get choked when some black cat
accuses me of racism for hirin' white players.
Some figure I should always give
a brother a leg-up. But I don't give a fuck
if a musician is red, blue, or purple —
as long as the motherfucker can play.

I didn't skitter; I didn't shuffle —
Sure as fuck I ain't gonna skeddaddle.
It'll take more than a conk on the coconut
to get this mo' fugger to move on —
and I ain't standin' in one spot either
doin' softshoe for any strawboatin' rube.

KIND OF BLUE

KIND OF BLUE (1959)

Such a delicate, transitory melody —
a sketch, or, no, a Japanese sumi
ink painting. The artist has only
a few fine brush hairs, one long
fluid state to get the essence
of beast or fowl, mountain or tree branch
down on the parchment,
must not hesitate or lift his hand
in the execution of the cipher image
or the parchment will tear, the fabric
of the dream, the mood, the very
reason for the piece will be lost.

So with the blues, these modal changes.
The pianist dips his fingers
in the keyboard stream, tickles the
ivory throats of minnows. The bassist
leans patiently over the ripples,
his big hands, strong spatulate fingers
plucking first one string then another,
placing each note just so, hanging back
a great blue heron standing statuesque
above the notes, choosing each with
lightning speed as the trumpet and sax
croon and lift their supple throats
to bolt down the fish they're fed and
rim shots come quick quick as rain
going pitter pat on the cymbal roof.

The whole pool shimmers, quivers
and the trumpet glissandos water strider
feet dance on the surface tension,
walking right out there on new waters,
graceful and fleeting as a mayfly

who in twenty-four short hours
will have played out the quiet drama
of its entire life. Such grace, such confidence —
You knew, you had to know that each take
would be the last, each track the imprint
of a behemoth in wax, a fossil record
of the passing of a wondrous beast
that would have its way with you
and carry you by the scruff of your neck
like some errant cub that had once again
broken away from the rest of the pride
made great strides for such plush feet.

Five tunes, five sunshine sketches,
five birds on the telephone wires,
five shots that would hold the silence
of a feather falling slowly ever after
and fix it like a fossil in wax forever
and change the very clay you stepped in.

CONCERTO DE ARANJUEZ
(*from* Sketches of Spain)

Joaquin would be pleased
> *his* canto hondo *reaches*
>> *greater heights than the trees.*

Joaquin would be pleased.
> *You could be Andalusian gypsies,*
>> *your trumpet: God's own guitar.*

Joaquin would be pleased.
> *You lift us all on a breeze*
>> *up from our knees.*

Rodrigo, put down your guitar.
> *Listen! There are crickets*
>> *in those castanets!*

Mountains, valleys, whole landscapes
> *implode in a stroke*
>> *of Gil Evan's baton!*

How far do we travel?
> *From whence do we arrive*
>> *riding such a plaintive sigh?*

Joaquin Rodrigo, savant/seer,
> *how much nearer to God*
>> *is the orchestra now?*

How much deeper is the dream
> *squeezed through*
>> *three little valves?*

Again, again we begin
> *the slow tympanic march*
>> *to the outer reaches of the heart.*

THE LETTER

We were too hot to stop!
My father gave me a letter.
I put it in my breast pocket.
It sat there for three days.

The phone call came while we
were doing a gig in K.C.
J.J. came up to me
and broke the bitter news.

All I could say was
No shit! Aw, goddamn!
Man, it was only then
I remembered the letter.

I'll never forget my father's
way of saying goodbye:
words shaky box cars trailing
behind the sad heart's wail:

"After your read this, I'll be dead,
so take care of yourself, Miles,"
he said, like he was leaving
on a business trip. So hip, so cool.

"I truly loved you, and you
made me proud." Only I
didn't feel so proud then
to have missed his eyes' intent.

My father's eyes were tunnels
from which emerged a train.
He was in the rear window waving.
I was going the other way.

SONNY ROLLINS' CALLIN'
(December 1962, Chicago)

Sonny wants to take the helm
of his own ship of fools,
woodsheds in the girders
high atop the Brooklyn Bridge.

He's like Bird — up there
in his music, all alone.
He's callin' to his maker
by long distance saxophone.

I know Sonny. He was my
running mate. He'd crank
the sun's rays if he could,
flag all that red sky

on the horizon and be
beatific and beautiful
as he pushed the plunger home,
Yeah. God is Sonny's real jones.

THE COMPLETE LIVE AT THE PLUGGED NICKEL
(Chicago, 1965)

Finally! The new stallion
is out of the stable!
It canters, prances, gallops
through time and changes,
like the sleek thoroughbred
you groomed so long for this.

> We were stretchin' out on the modal thing.
> Folks dug the swing, the easy loping grace,
> how we served up blues without thick chords,
> the straightjacket of thirty-two bars.

No need to run the melody
like horse meat through the grinder!
No need to play the head,
then give each man his solo
like a bucket of oats! These cats
aren't Clydesdales you need to yoke.

> The white crickets had been so busy
> lookin' for a new place on their legs to saw
> they'd pushed free jazz over the edge,
> were reduced to chirpin' in a closet.

Your chops are down, but not your wit,
your joy, your hard intelligence,
or sense of adventure. No! You trot
while Herbie comps and Ron strides,
Tony kicks up tufts of grass with each
symbol splash. Wayne's tenor weaves,
each note a honey bee in clover.

Trane was the voice of rage
to the Panthers and angry blacks
and everyone was chantin' "Burn, baby, burn!"
while we were put on some back burner.

A ballad's suddenly a flag waver,
then a head-bobbin' groover,
the whole band's racing toward
the headlight of a train, galloping
at a full clip along the tracks,
mane flying like some World War I
ace's scarf. We want to shout woah!

Jazz lost its broad appeal to rock.
The British Invasion copped its chops
from black R & B, so these Mods
sounded half-assed new, half-assed hip.

Think of Isadora's scarf
racing out behind a roadster
until it got caught in the rear spokes
and strangled her. But no —
the head's already gone. You're up
in the stratosphere, not ridin' stallion at all!

Suddenly that sorry-assed Doris Day shit
has its skirt up way past the knees.
Elvis and Jerry Lee are slippin'
a whole new generation of boppers the bone.

Your Lamborghini is screaming down
the highway, the segmented white line
disappearing like tracer fire into the windshield,
the labyrinthine streets of your brain
on a night full of stars, the high speed
dental whine of cicadas in the trees.

86

It ain't nothin' but amplified blues
and simple three-chord attitude.
They had a perforated president and Nam
til they did Malcolm and King.

You're cruising in a well-tuned machine,
metaphor sparking in all the cylinders.
Take the old book and all the
unexpected curves at a devilish clip,
climbing some cliff-side highway,
ascend the seven steps it takes
to get to heaven. Take us for the ride!

Bloods were disappearin' off the block,
comin' home in boxes in bigger numbers
than white rich kids for years.
Still, the Kennedys had started something.

Down shifting's a breeze. Top's down
as you tool into cool,
big fat bass notes percolating on
some back burner of the store.
Down home and funky now. Ain't no
backwoods preacher can deliver the news
and fill the pews the way you do.

The military-industrial complex was tumblin'
with the death of those white boys
and Malcolm and King, for all their differences,
had turned some kind of blue-eyed tide.

We're back on the farm.
Out for a jaunt on a string of ponies
that make us the boss posse of the bop
perimeter. Tony's cymbals go
chicka chick and we mosey along,
lookin' over hill and dale for all
the lost lambs of this world.

> Trane was playin' love-ins for white folks.
> Les Paul cranked up the volume some,
> but I had these badass new bloods
> showin' me electricity. I'd turn the corner —

Such beauty can't last. In each wail
of your harmon mute we hear the bray
of lost animals. Would that such music
could call us all home, but it can't.
You can't. The band can't, though each
note chuffs along like the engine that could.

> take the motherfuckers back to Main Street
> cos there ain't been no drummer like Tony
> to get a fire under my ass. No bassist
> like Ron Carter to keep us in the pocket.

Four nights. Seven sets. Eight sides.
No two takes of the same tune alike.
What a ride! You hit the sixties
full stride, with psychedelia and
Teo Macero's splicing of your long
fusion jams still around the corner.
Take us downtown, Miles!

Wayne was a badass free horn player
who liked to play within the forms.
He composed like a motherfucker too
and Herbie could do anything he could do.

Whirl like Wurlitzer dervishes!
Play your book forwards, backwards, blind!
In the studio you align new racks
of test tubes and flasks. This is the autoclave,
the secret laboratory of the heart,
the retort where jazz alchemy's defined!
Here our molecules are re-aligned.

This quintet would blow the doors off
my Cannonball-Trane quintet,
I just knew it. We got so tight
we were a different band every night.

MILES SMILES (1966)

1. "Orbits"

*Improvising on open horn
in straight hard bop form —
to hell with the rock audience:
this is still an acoustic
jazz outing. Your chops
are strong. You climb
the gyre, glide in patient
circles as your sidemen,
one by one, come into
orbit with you. The earth
so abstract, a geometric
pattern of overlapping
rectangles from up there.*

2. "Circle"

*Muted, and quieter now:
Tony on brushes: each
note like the falling
of a single water droplet
in a pond. The ripples
flow out in concentric
circles, each image
in the mercuric surface
of the water softened,
eventually obliterated.*

3. "Footprints"

*You are walking on
an emotional sandbar.
Everywhere the ground is firm
but each step you take*

wells up with water,
becomes its own little lake.
Where can such footprints
lead but to the bottom
of a deep, cold sea?
Simple, you say, I'll
walk on the backs of
flying fishes as they
breach each incoming wave
and stride out to another
musical reef, another island
in an archipelago of needs.

4. "Dolores"
What kind of face do you give
a woman in love with such
abstract beauty? Is she a city girl
given to exploring rectilinear
quadrants of desire, or is she
a country girl whose curvaceous
lines echo the landscape into
which she was born? You go looking
for her with your questing blue horn,
but she is not someone you
can recognize by merely eliciting
a smile.
Her smiles, like the Mona
Lisa's, impute other affairs,
a deep-seated contentment
and wisdom that is always
on the other shore from the
place you beach your canoe.

5. *"Freedom Jazz Dance"*

A lazy summer day
when you don't have to
get up and go to work.

The kind of day you'd
drive if you could take
it anywhere. Here and now

having become too familiar,
too much like a house
full of comfortable furniture,

but the saxophone is
beginning to natter on
about something of consequence,

and you aren't listening.
The piano cuts in the way
a river cuts into a bank.

The very architecture of desire,
the house in which thought resides,
is constantly being undermined.

You want to take off
your clothes, dance naked
before the mirror,

but the mirror no longer
tells you the lies you've
programmed into it.

You start detaching limbs,
breasts, buttocks. Nothing
you feed it staves off its hunger.

It is like a deep pool
that is home to a monster.
Everything that touches its surface

dances briefly on the surface
tension before a huge fish
comes up to swallow it.

You can't find the right words
to trick it into swallowing
any hook or teaser.

It's old as Methuselah,
so large it might swallow
the whole boat of longing.

6. "Ginger Bread Boy"

The ginger bread boy
has escaped the oven
and is beating a path
to the local constabulary.

When he gets there he'll
accuse you of all kinds
of heinous acts, not the least
of which is not adding sugar.

The problem as he sees it
is getting there in one piece
when he has to leave crumbs
the birds eat in following him.

How can he find his way back
to the delightful cottage
in the woods where the poor
woodsman and his wife live?

How can he convince anyone
he's real when he's used up
all his legs and arms to get
away without being eaten?

MILES IN THE SKY (1967)

1. "Stuff"

Strutting your stuff over the bad back beat
of Tony Williams' cymbal and snare
splashes, Herbie's funky electric piano
meanderings, you stroll past the bop
landscape like a new Realtor confident
in the development he must sell a banker.
Stuff — not fusion, but some wry musings,
enough to fill a mattress with, to fluff up
a pillow to. Stuff — not a tune but fragments
of melody that will crop up later in your
architectural wanderings. Good stuff, useful —
like the concentric circles of colour you let
represent the bell of your trumpet that on
the cover metamorphose into a butterfly.

2. "Paraphernalia"

Your first session with electric guitar.
George Benson handles the honours,
at first confining himself to quiet riffs
behind Herbie's piano. Rhythm, not lead.
And, like Johnny Appleseed, you
are out there on terra firma
sowing fertile ground, pulling back
on the shaft of the shovel to make
a "V", stamping the ground to close
the gap once the seed is planted.
I don't know what paraphernalia
you thought you needed, but when George
decides to pipe up it's as though a
mother quail were calling her children
out from under the brush. The notes

are timorous, don't strike out on a
bold course of their own.
Even Herbie pecks like a chicken
in Thelonious Monk's old henhouse.

3. "Black Comedy"

Is that comedy by black comedians
for black consumption or comedy so sick
it's funny? It's hard to put the metaphor
to music so abstract, so deliberately
undeliberated. Is that irony or mama
doin' the ironin'? No matter: it's
a sunny day and Herbie's fingers
are flyin' like a witty conversation.
The repartee and sparkle of wit
has all the sheets hung out to dry.

4. "Country Son"

This country boy has gone uptown
to Orleans on his horn. Ain't about
to be 'buked or scorned for his rube
or cube-like ways. He's gawkin'
from the sidewalk, maybe has his
straw boater pushed back way too far
from his forehead, but there
sure enough are some sights to see.
The women are so sexy, so slinky
the way they swish in and out of
doorways. Every note wears a tight
skirt too. Even commerce can be sexy.

But the mind wanders when the sky
is so blue and clouds all look
like teddy bears. You want to walk
down the street with your neck
craning at all the tall buildings,
rubberneck at ideas deking
into every side street,
every back alley.

JAPANESE WOMEN

They stand at
the edge of your
field of vision

just where you can
see them out of the
corner of your eye.

They'll be there
if they're interested —
almost out of sight.

Won't look at you
directly, say dick
or get in your face.

They're like angels,
ghost notes floating
on the edge of a prayer.

If there are four
Japanese women
hovering near you like that

and you speak to one,
the others will
dissipate like smoke.

I love that.
It's so beautiful,
so coo-oo-l.

I think maybe
a trumpet solo
ought to be like that:

a smoke ring halo
floated just over
your noble head.

ELEGY FOR JOHN COLTRANE
(d. July 17, 1967)

I didn't know.
How could I have known?
You weren't feeling well, sure.
You were overweight, maybe.
Hadn't been playin' on stage, OK

I thought you were woodshedding again.
Were there no more Pharaohs
to take you to the source of all your Niles?
No more prayers like "Ascension",
"Meditations" or "A Love Supreme"?

You've combined all
those sheets of sound
into one big OM.
Intone your mantra, John.
Say it isn't so.

No one could blow like you!
You left Shepp and Gilmore
for the upper stratosphere,
orbited Ganymede,
sowing your soprano seed.

Blow, Trane, blow!
Say it isn't so!
I loved you, man!
More when you were
playing beside me —

but I never meant you
to take your final bow —
certainly not offstage, quietly.
It wasn't your way!
You should have raged, Trane, raged!

You shred earth's molecules,
split the last infinitesimal atom
of the last thirty-second note,
were the star cloak of Andromeda!
How could you just leave?

Cirrhosis of the liver?
When you were so clean and pure?
Maybe you were too good for this earth.
Did you only mean to take a peak
beneath the final sheet of sound?

Were you just stepping behind the curtain
for another reed? To find some pristine
washroom where the porcelain gave back
a cleaner sound? Did you find
another interval between the notes?

"BANG, YOU'RE DEAD, MOTHERFUCKER!"

October '69, the band and I
had just finished a gig
at the Blue Coronet in Brooklyn.

I had driven my new flame,
Marguerite, back to her place.
We were parked alongside the curb.

We were mindin' our business,
just talkin', kissin' a bit —
you know, doin' stuff lovers do —

This car with three black dudes
pulls up next to mine.
I don't pay it much mind.

I'm thinkin' maybe these guys
had heard us at the club,
just wanted to say hi.

I turn to acknowledge them
when — bang, bang, bang . . .
one cat squeezes off his load.

Shit! My left side stings
but I'm too shocked
to be scared. My eyes are wide.

The fuckers peel out,
are halfway up the block
before I know what's happened.

There musta been five holes
in the side of my Ferrari,
but they missed Marguerite.

I would have bit it
right then and there,
but I was wearin' a leather coat.

It was long and loose-fitting.
It and that fine-crafted door
musta slowed down the bullets some.

But — what the fuck —
I didn't have a damn clue
who these chuckleheads were —

let alone why the motherfuckers
wanted to put my black ass
in the freakin' cold ground.

Marguerite's freaked too,
but we manage to get inside
and call the cops.

Two white dicks show up
and start to search my car!
Claim to find some tea to boot!

Now anyone who knows me
knows I don't like marijuana
and never liked to toke.

So this is some sad fucker's
bad idea of a joke.
Pure harassment, nothin' else.

They just didn't figger
no fine-dressed nigger
could be with such a fine woman —

and own a Ferrari —
unless he was a pimp
or drug dealer or somethin'.

The honky yokels didn't approve
of such a light-skinned beauty
swappin' spit with me is all.

Eventually though I got the story.
Some black promoters were pissed
that I hadn't cut them in.

White promoters were handling
all my bookings, so I must be
some Jim Crow motherfucker.

Like I need to get it
up the ass from an angry brother!
Man, life is a bitch sometimes!

Anyway, I offered five grand
for information. A few weeks later
learn the cat who popped me's dead.

The cat who told me
didn't tell me the shooter's name.
Only that the jiveass got his back.

Someone on the street
didn't approve of the treatment
I'd received and got even.

But now this story follows me around
of how I hired a hit man,
am suddenly The Prince of Darkness.

Man, I'm a nigger scorned, yet again.
All I ever had to say
I've said through my black horn.

But shit clings to you, you know.
And my past ain't never goin' away.
I'm the junky pimp trumpet player.

I gotta be some badass super dude
to deflect bullets and keep my
black ass outta jail.

Man, what's a motherfucker to do
when white folks keep playin'
that sorry ol' tune?

BITCHES BREW

MARIJUANA

I never liked Mary Jane,
but they'd throw me her panties
whenever I played to rock crowds
at the Avalon or Fillmore ballrooms.

She just makes me nod;
she doesn't have the kick of horse
or light up my circuit boards.
I always saw her as a cheap whore.

I'm not gonna put my million dollar lips
on no cheap two-dollar pussy
and suckin' on her makes my
throat sore. She don't inspire me.

I got nothin' against her though.
If she makes some freckle-faced
farmer from the sticks sit up
and take notice of my music, great.

Maybe he'll put his twangy shit away,
let his hair grow, get down
and get some real chicken grease
on those tuberous fingers of his.

I don't smoke to find
the rosy haze around places
my music takes me.
I want it all up in your body.

Like Dali said when the hippies
asked him if he took LSD,
"I don't need to take hallucinogenic drugs;
I am a hallucinogenic drug!"

Everything pours into the vortex
of my horn and finds its form
in the tiny detonations of breath
I control with lips and fingers.

I don't want to burn like a slow fuse
that ends in the lungs instead
of the heart. I don't want to smolder
like the butt-ends of hazy days.

I want to focus your energy
like a laser beam, cut through the steel
of this century with a will
and sound pure as oxyacetylene.

IN A SILENT WAY (1969)

1. "In A Silent Way"

In a silent way
        in a quiet way
                the way one plays
a peaceful lullaby

In a silent way
        in a quiet way
                the way an ocean liner
slips out into the bay

In a silent way
        in a quiet way
                the way one says goodbye
to a continent, a language, a culture

In a silent way
        in a quiet way
                with a lump in the throat
the last swallow of sadness and grief

In a silent way
        in a quiet way
                the way a tramp steamer
brings a sea-weary sailor home

You nudge the electric prow
        of fusion slowly
                into acoustic waters
and breathe deep the salt sea air.

2. "It's About That Time"

It's about time
     about space
          about the hoarse whisper
recorded as you set the pace

It's about time
     about rhythm
          the simple but insistent
sound of drumsticks, brushes
sweeping out a place

about time simple ostinato riffs
     soprano sax, organ, bass
laying down a watercolour wash
     the tentative phrases
and bold brash strokes
     of your trumpet
saying yes, yes
     it's time for a change
     it's time I staked a claim
     it's time I slipped
in a silent way
     in a quiet way
          right into place.

3. "Shh/Peaceful"

Shh / Peaceful: the tune
     full of moonlight
          and silver water

you stretch out in this
     free form electric wash
          take us to the river

So melodic, so propulsive
   under the cymbal splash
     of Tony Williams' brushes

The current rushes, eddies
   in deep dark pools
     the moon a blue canoe

BITCHES BREW (1969)

1. *"Pharaoh's Dream": Improvisation # 1*
It's churning under the surface of the beat
a moiling, roiling electricity looking to be free
from the puppies whelped from the underbelly
of acoustic piano's European melodies
a funkier rhythm than jazz had hitherto known
the notes of Maupin's bass clarinet noodling
nosing like alley cats, overturning cans
while the backbeat reaches a full rolling boil
in hell's kitchen and the electric piano riffs
stab and poke like egrets at the sands
of the Nile. *"Pharaoh's Dance"*, a mad
free coupling of the first two amphibians
to pull the saxophone's mournful belly cries
to the shore of the new continent, the new hope.

The electric piano and drums are having a conversation
while Shorter's sax entreats us to remember John
and Ravi in the loose shambling unraveling of
limbs and Miles' horn — cool, ethereal as always —
sprinkles notes like stars about the inky canopy
above the seas where evolution is making up its
collective improvisational mind about what to
do with McLaughlin's upstart guitar riffing and chopping
through the primordial soup — finny wings flashing
like flying fish. More honoured in the breach than
in the practice of the melody.

Then muteless Miles soars and the whole primordial
soup simmers down to a low boil percolates
its java jive and the sprightly electric piano notes
cavort otter-like in the sun-dappled waves sea
to shining sea. Something rises from the bottom making

low mournful cries like a new whale whelped of
but suckling its child.

A stew of influences — bebop, impressionism,
the structured free jazz that was to answer
Ornette's squeak, squawk, honk, blat, bleep
and enter the ghost of the machine's new
unspoken vocabulary. What is this bitch
this female dog older than time? What
is it she has whelped and what fur is
this glistening under moonlight on the River
Nile? What strange beast slouching toward
what new Bethlehem of the senses?

2. "*Bitches Brew*": *Improvisation # 2*

Chicka chicka chicka boom boom thump —
not quite that lumpy or lumbering a start.
Cool as a swagger he steps into the music.
What? What? says the horn and
can you dig this? What I'm saying. What is happening
in the long interval between the brights
of sprightly conversation and that bullfrog bass
clarinet breathes through its pores.

I'm high hattin' confident now. See hear:
this is the New Jerusalem — my streets
I'm stridin' down. What? Who? the
high notes ask. Come in. I'll show you
what it means to be all these streets
meeting under the starry dynamo of Blake
and yer new white boy Ginsberg's Howl.
That tenement over there. This warehouse.
Those stars shining over all. Listen to
the hollow body Gibson talk of electric cat guts
on metal strings singing to its own hollow
belly and rib-thin bloated stomach.
Listen to the tenor sax and bass clarinet
as the former strokes the silky fur of the latter
in some corner where the Master in silk red
white piped pajamas sits.

Two cats in heat vie for the same bitch kitten here.
The long low wail of the dispossessed
clinging to the furniture the landlord
has had hauled from the belly of

some walk-up Brownstone's dry heave
of interiors here. And more of the cosmos
in the hollow ravening belly of the notes
than you have ever known. Don't
lose the beat it says. Keep time it says.

Come outside. The sun is bright the
street lamps only late last night illumined
with the promise of some unknown blue note
now a globe a cluster of grapes just now
ripe for the picking. Say what? What?
Pick me. Oh, pick me there, handsome.
Let me step lively beside you to some
curb of consciousness. You have the vehicle.
You have all the pretty black notes to
string like laundry between buildings —
so many discrete crisp clean clear notes
that even music is a kind of currency
you can keep warming your backside
and billfold with. Come. Step lively.
The music wills it.

Now we're on the other side of the River Lethe.
The city looks like a crushed corsage from here
and I want to speak to you softly now.
Calmly. Away from the kliegs and
interrogation of the other instruments
embroiled in the battle it took to get here.
I want to say you are safe on this new shore.
You have always been safe. Each clear
soprano note a petal on the flower I pick for
you saying I love you? I love you not.
This is a very old dance the Pharaoh has
enacted for us. A very old

dance in the loose shambling and entwining
of limbs that leaves us beached on the
far shore of consciousness. We do it urgently
as though tomorrow were yesterday and
Bird did not die for our sins and
Coltrane had had enough of meditation and booze
and smack to settle down into the furniture
of all our knowing and recognized home
for the very first time. Do you understand?
It is the only question the trumpet bell of
this gold flower ever asks of the sky. And
it has rained last night. The air is suddenly
free of impurities just as the music is.
We can sort among the notes for that sweet ambrosia
that is all the notes all the words we'll ever need.

The ship has docked. All the tired babushkaed
women and their children are ashore. It's dawn
again for the first time. You can feel it in
the sugar that replaces the lactic acid lassitude
of tired limbs, can you not? I'm here for you
for you for you the notes keep reminding us.
Can't hear it! Can't hear it! Can hear
no more cacophony, only the ambrosia of the
spaces between the notes now.

A TRIBUTE TO JACK JOHNSON (1970)

1. *"Right Off"*

Right off the top, screaming
    in whitey's face
        just like Jack

Right off the funk groove
    wailing aggressive blues
        just like Jack

Smilin' to their faces
    walkin' the streets of Paris
        drinking the best champagne

Right off the mark
    driving fast cars
        smokin' fat cigars

Right to the floor
    screamin' I ain't poor
        white women on his tail —

or lookin' for it
    wah wah wailin' America's pain
        in being born black

and seein' white
    for sanitized sheets
        the racist mothers wore

Right to the bridge
    cryin' Cro Magnon's
        heavy brow ridge

and thinking heads don't
    get any thicker
        than these cats'

who wanted him
        to take a dive or die
                while he beat sense

into all of us
        pounding the walls
                pounding pavement

Right off the top
        of the heavyweights' roster
                into the clouds

Surrounded by admirers
        and hangers on
                thumpin' on his bass

to get at the waste
        of all that racist jazz
                not buyin' no razzmatazz

until he bought the farm
        at sixty-eight
                crashing one of his cars

Right off the mark
        just like you, a dentist's son
                with teeth that chewed leather

and grit behind the embouchure
        of tough cheek and hard gaze
                the way you spent your days

Jack Johnson, heavyweight champion
        of this or any 1908 world
                that balances a feather

on the hard funk of electric guitar
the documentary fist
or calloused upper lip

Right off the top
resounding, resolved to knock
us flat to the mat.

2. "Yesternow"

All the pensive yesterdays
we carry as luggage
to the edge of sorrow

All the nows disappearing
as boats carrying lost loves
over the horizon

All the hopes and glories
that fit thought's
turned out pockets

All the dreams that drowned
in a glass of champagne
before memories' sad refrain —

an excerpt of "In A Silent Way"
spliced into the mix
of slow wah wah talkin' —

Your inimitable caught-in-the-throat cry
of all the lost and lonely
waving their goodbyes

The sound of butterflies crying
one inflated tear sliding
from cheek to pavement

All the phase shifters, echo
　　　reverb and other
　　　　　electronic devices used

to bring Telemusik from
　　　deep space to the
　　　　　intervals between words:

"I'm Jack Johnson
　　　Heavyweight Champion
　　　　　of the world!

I'm black. They never let me forget it.
　　　I'm black all right —
　　　　　I never let them forget it."

AT JIMI'S GRAVE

Jimi, you scare me, man!
With your Strat and that
big bank of Marshall amps,
we would have razed the ground!

Your "Machine Gun" mowed us down!
That sound pinned Nam, Nixon,
the whole Dixon / chitlin' circuit thang
to the killin' floor! What could I do?!

The suits are still cryin' uncle!
You had me run my voodoo down —
after you turned the anthem inside out —
I had to go to Africa to find you, man!

We could have nuked Osaka —
knocked everything standing flat!
As it is, my scorched horn goes searchin'
like some kind of alley cat for scraps.

Cosey and Lucas are motherfuckers —
don't get me wrong. I'm lucky to
have both of them runnin'
search-and-destroy missions for me —

but a paratrooper who turned the blues purple?!
The guy whose strangled notes were waterfalls
that cleansed us all? You have to know
Agharta and *Pangaea* were for you, babe.

I wanted you in my band so bad!
I didn't give a flyin' Philly
that you couldn't read the music, man!
I was recording. It just seemed easier

to drop off some sheet music
at the party, you know. Now folks
are hissin' like sprinklers on summer lawns,
sayin' I didn't want you in my crib.

It's bullshit, man! I dug you
as much as I dug Duke, Bird, Trane —
all them bad dudes with attitude.
I could have set up currents for you.

You would have glided, soared,
blitzed the shit outta everything alive
cos there's no purple haze flare flaggin'
you home, baby; you burst through the stratosphere!

Left us standin' around some headstone,
lookin' up! Do you hear me, Jimi?
When I get there, man — you, me, Bird, Trane —
we're gonna make some awful noise!

Gil too. Cos your moves and God
and Gil's own blue orchestra
are gonna fill miles of aisles on cloud nine.
We've got a date, babe; don't be late!

LIVE EVIL (1970)

Purists were pissed. Some abandoned you
after Filles . . . your last acoustic set.
Others hung in for the moody tone poems
of In a Silent Way, *the fusion of* Bitches Brew.

But the cacophony, electrified density,
muddy mix of your live Fillmore sets
claimed more casualties. Haight-Ashbury
wasn't a bopper's gig. Why the harlequin?

Now this?! Your name spelled backward?!
Electric hiccoughs, muted wah wah riffs?!
You might as well have farted through
your horn, according to former sidemen.

You've blasphemed in the House of Bop!
Left washers on the floor of modal and cool!
Bring Stockhausen to Sly? James Brown
to Bop? Electronic razzmatazz to free jazz?

"Funky Tonk"? "Sivad"? "Nem Um Talvez"?
Where's the monkey with the red velvet fez
now that you're grinding out fat organ chords?
What's the gospel according to your "Little Church"?

What's this pagan, funky shit? Not jazz —
or is it? The bass vamps are infectious.
They cants stop they feets. They's commenced
to jumping in the aisles. "What [You] Say," Miles!

Gotta get down. Out of the clouds and down
on solid black ground. Pavement's the way:
the vortex of your horn the Scylla and Charybdis
of Black America's seas. Selim Sivad, you're bad!

Scream pterodactyl raptor grief! Fly high
in any key. Take us to the forest primeval,
compress the vegetation down to fossil fuel
in each valve of your black ammonite horn.

Pump it up! Pump it up! Get up with the
low growl of gospel organ, the shriek and shred
of psychedelic acid raptor guitar. Give us
music for the head by way of booty and balls.

Give us funky tonk monkey talk. Street lean
supreme. Swing us high in your funky vines.
Take us to the top of the funk-jazz canopy
so we can see the mountains you bring to Mohammed.

Sanctify Ray Charles, Rahsaan, and Duke
with your dukes up. Those of us weaned on
the Animals, Jimi, the Airplane and Dead
got no problem with wedding Karlheinz to Sly.

Give us frightening runs of electric shred acid blues
and distortion. Cry like the first baby born
to Nefertiti in Egypt. Overflow your Niles!
Black Magus, Miles, put us on trial for our lives.

Hear the beating of blood in the temples. The
low funk thud of bass in the blood. Pump
it up! Patch the tired ol' inner tube walls
of embolised art. Shoot adrenaline into the heart.

We want drum solos! Gospel moan down
in the guts. Sho' nuff dem muses got vulvas.
Stuff they muffins with blue marrow bones.
Get they up. Get they up to answer they phones.

Live evil lives. One size don't be fittin' all.
Play evil lines. Entwine vines all shapes
and size. Live outsized lives. Spotlight the lies.
Live evil lives. Play in and out of funk time.

ON THE CORNER (1972)

Turn on the fire hydrants!
The Street's a skillet,
the catfish notes are jumpin'!

That cat in his fedora
he gotta borra
a double sawbuck.

That big butt mama
ain't just coolin'
her keister on a stump.

Two cats in afros,
flared bellbottoms
and platform shoes

be givin' each other
low fives, bobbin'
and weavin' in the street.

The music from
the brother's boom box
is so uptown hip

so down and funky
ain't a junky usin'
that ain't noddin' approval.

This ain't suit music
Miles be wailing through
his cry baby pedal.

Some skunk funk!
This music is free
like water from a hydrant.

The kids don't got no
suburban lawn or
Rainbird to run through.

They got what they take.
This music is their music —
hard as a monkey wrench.

I HAD A WHITE WOMAN DEALER

One time I didn't have no dough.
I went over to her place
to pick up some coke.
I was buyin' a lot of shit from her,
always paid the bitch what I owed.

She was stone cold. Gave me the once-over,
said, "No money, no cocaine, Miles."
Wouldn't budge. The doorman called
upstairs to tell her her boyfriend
was on his way up. I asked her again.

She stood her ground, so I went
into her bedroom, took off my clothes.
I knew that her old man knew
I had a rep for bein' a ladies man.
She started beggin' me to leave.

I just lay on her bed with my
dick in one hand and my other
hand held out for the dope.
Grinned at the bitch 'til she relented.
She cursed me up and down and sideways

but I got my dope before I
got dressed and got out of there.
When the elevator opened
her boyfriend stepped out
with a funny look on his face.

It was the kinda look that said
"Has this nigger been with my old lady?"
I wanted to smirk, gyrate my hips
for the motherfucker, but I just
nodded and I never went back.

ANOTHER SNOWFALL IN AUGUST

Once I had run out of coke.
We were gettin' on a plane
to go to some concert somewhere.

I thought Jackie was holdin',
started goin' through her purse.
Came across a package of Woolite.

After I tasted the shit
I was one embarrassed mother.
Folks were starin' like I was nuts.

Ever try to snort detergent?
Maybe I shoulda that time.
I mighta got whiter than white.

BREAKING UP WITH MARGUERITE

Marguerite was so beautiful
people would follow her in galleries
as if she was the work of art.

The last time we made love
she got pregnant with Erin.
I said I'd stay with her.

"You want us to be members
of your entourage," she said.
"We're not roadies, Miles.

I'm not another statuette.
You can't square off my ass
with any kind of frame."

I respected that. She went her way.
Now I'm my family's own curator,
hang family portraits like a show.

SILENCE

SILENCE

For six friggin' years
I didn't pick up my horn —
not once, though I frequently
approached and circled it the way
a hyena circles a dying lion.

Oh! It looked like food
and I really wanted to play,
but all the music had bled it out of me
like blood from a store-bought steak.

I was forty-nine.
Music had been all I lived for
since I was a kid of thirteen.
I needed a break, I needed a change;
needed to put my life back together again.

My hip was giving me grief.
I limped like a wounded animal on stage,
could no longer pace the cage of my bones
or endure the pitying stares of the audience
that came to watch me bugle my pain.

Artie Shaw had told me years before
I couldn't play the third concert in bed,
and I was already feeling half-past dead,
so I made the bedroom my stage.

I became the sole performer and only audience
to my pain. Spent up to $500 a day on cocaine
before I got my snoot full. Ate more chicken,
chitterlings, and funky pussy than any man
has a right to put greasy chin to.

I didn't listen to the music
and when I didn't have blow
my temper grew short.
I'd take pills, so I could sleep —
but I didn't want to sleep,
and started prowlin' the streets
like a damn vampire.

Bein' a Gemini, I was already two people,
but back then I was four:
two people on coke; two off.
Two with consciences; two without.
I'd be up for four days, would hallucinate
and do weird shit. The maid stayed away.
My thoughts were roaches, skittering
from dirty dishes to the dirty dog.

The suits and band mates came around, at first,
but I slammed the door too many times.
Then my sister's boy, Vincent, came to visit,
and bashed around on the traps
I gave him when he was seven,
asked me questions about music all the time
to pry me out of my clam.

Then Cicely started lookin' in on me,
gradually hauled my ass back from the dead
by feedin' me vegetables 'n' vitamins 'n' shit.
I tapered off the snow and sleeping pills;
switched from cognac to rum and Coke;
eventually, quit the Heinekens and cigarettes.
(She wouldn't kiss no compost.)

She kicked out the bitches, and my senses kicked in.
I'd been livin' in sin for six years, some say,
but I didn't see it that way. No.
I was some coked out Casanova
greasin' my pole 'n' fine flared nose
in every woman I could take home.
I thought life was a Lamborghini!

Yeah, I was so hep to get to the third act,
I kept my foot on the accelerator
until I wrapped her 'round a pole,
but I was a charmed motherfucker too,
and when I came to, my trumpet sat grinnin'
like the grill of a new car in the showroom.
I smelled new leather, baby, I smelled leather!

COCAINE

The snow is so cold this year.
I can feel ice crystals
forming behind my eyes.

At first a snort or two
would turn on all the lights.
I lit up like a Christmas tree.

Now it's more like the panel
of a Boeing 747:
there are so many switches to trip.

The landing gear is down.
I can see the running lights,
but I cannot connect the dots.

Somewhere inside my mad circuitry
a little black box
is supposed to be recording this.

I raise the trumpet to my lips.
My fans, you are at the wrong end
of a pair of binoculars —

You are so far away
and I am moving so fast
I am running into my own notes.

If I crash and burn,
a record of the flakes will remain.
Under a microscope no two will look alike.

MEMPHIS IN THE MEANTIME

Doodling with a set of felt pens
on a drawing pad, the delicate
curves that might have been
the choice few plangent notes
of another solo or laconic remark
start to form the shapely booty
or ample boobs of another muse,
mutate into the picayunish pixie
or snake that coils its flaccid
question elsewhere on the page.
A game of exquisite corpse becoming
a kind of automatic writing for
two or four hands, what you do
instead of blowing smoke rings
at the hotel ceiling, snorting coke,
or looking for an unused vein,
or stray piece of ass to get you
through another day, while your
lacquered horn branches into
another perch for the rare avis
to light on when you can't
bring yourself to reach for it,
so the blue fuse that through
the valves and tubing that once
blossomed in rare orchids on
your lips, flows down through
your hands, into your fingertips
and sips a little like a
hummingbird from the same
rich bell of the flower that is
the source, and you ask
Mike Zwerin, an alumnus from
the Cool days, if he likes these chicks.

Say these are Parisian women,
their sunken cheeks obtained naturally
from speaking with their tongues out
and retreating behind yet another
rueful grin as you intone
the verdict that language —
language forms your face,
your own chiseled self portrait
wearing a lone ranger mask
to cover the eyes while the trumpet
becomes a series of abstract
forms and lines and your
hand never once leaves the page.

Why should we be so surprised —
that the demiurgic
force igniting the fuse
should light a flower
that others will want
to wear on their lapels?
You put down your horn
because you felt you had
nothing more to say,
and found another fluid
concourse to get from
the river that ran through you
to the mother of all seas.
Not the Atlantic or Pacific,
but Panthalassa,
the primordial ocean.
So the paint drips,
the lines slip and the
mask slips,
the mask slips.

FIRST STROKE

One night I was reaching for a cigarette
and found I couldn't close the fingers
of my right hand. "What the fuck is this?!"
I yelled. I was scared shitless.

I phoned Cicely. She said it sounded
like a stroke and flew right home.
I wanted to think I'd choked the chicken
one too many times and would soon be fine.

But I knew: this was payback for all the cigarettes,
the drug and alcohol abuse. See, I'd shot
a speedball into my leg a few days before.
That had fucked me up pretty badly too.

Soon I didn't even have the strength
to pee straight. I'd wobble like boney maroney,
astride that gleaming porcelain pony
and dribble all down my legs, for Christ's sake!

Couldn't even get up enough pressure to arc
one over the rim. My piss'd be bloody too.
I was shit scared. I'd never get to play
either of my two favourite instruments again.

Then the doctor said if I had sex
any time in the next six months
I could have another stroke, blow a gasket.
So there I lay for six fuckin' months.

I couldn't even one-hand rein my pony
off into the sunset. Had to just
watch the tent poles collapse while
all my good intentions broke camp.

This was the time my hair started
to blow away like tumbleweeds.
We're not talkin' pattern baldness —
it went by handfuls, clumps —

and I'm a vain motherfucker.
Always prided myself on lookin' clean.
And here I was: a scarecrow
scared of his own lengthening shadow.

LISTEN, WYNTON

Listen, Wynton, I know you're a badass player.
I don't begrudge you the kudos.
You've earned 'em, God knows.
You can blow the doors off my sorry ass,
but that don't give you the right
to dis me and Diz, let alone put down
your own bro' Brantford, as bad as he is.

You talk about tradition and roots,
but what about dues? Can't you see
those white crickets just want to egg you on
so they can jump all over you
when you miss a note? It ain't about
hittin' or missin' a friggin' note, man!
It's about the whole game plan.

Yeah, Classical music is great,
but it's dead white European music
and it's up in your head too much.
You need to feel the low rumble of rage
down in your stomach and in your balls.
You need to ask how come they ain't
studying Bird or Trane or Monk,
Tatum, Ellington, or Armstrong
in the academic system you praise.

I ain't one to piss on the roses.
I ain't no pedigree poodle.
But I ain't no mongrel mutt neither
lookin' to squat on some manicured lawn.
You gotta realize we got
an academy too, and you ain't
pissin' down on me from such a great height.

Improvise, improvise. You ain't
so shit hot that you gotta re-do hard bop
or perfect my cool. It ain't about
layin' down a perfect groove or
turning the past into some neoclassical repast.
It's about re-toolin' to create a new music —
our music. Black classical music.

The crickets will bury you in the press
if you press ahead, true. But you
don't want to be a footnote, shit hot as you are.
And while your star is in the ascendant,
you should be thinking of movin' ahead.

You want the critics to be one step behind,
not crowning your nappy black head,
or you are dead and already issued
a pine box to writhe in. They did me.
They've done others before me. They'll dis you.
Get used to it, Wynton. You're black.

Our music isn't the same on Friday
and Saturday night. Our food isn't theirs.
Real black people don't sit up there and listen
to Billy Graham and those sorry ass preachers.

It's like brother Malcolm said:
We didn't land on Plymouth Rock;
Plymouth Rock landed on our black asses.
You ain't hip, if you ain't hip to that.

THE MAMMY AWARDS

We should have Mammies, not Grammies.
We could have black musicians tearing up
their Mammy Awards right on television.
That'd be great. No more grittin' teeth,
sittin' and grinnin' while white cats
get the applause and fame for playin' black.
Mammy Awards. Yeah, that's the ticket.
Sho' nuff boss. You wan' a liddle skiffle
in the middle of your lunch, a little softshoe?
Gimme a Mammy Award. I'll get down
on one knee and raise one arm real high
and do Jolson for you. Mammy! Mammy!

JACKIE BATTLE

After Marguerite left me
Jackie became my main squeeze,
but I was still playin'
the jackass Romeo.

Jackie found some Polaroids
of naked women in nasty poses.
Holed up in her apartment,
pulled the phone jack from the wall.

So, yeah, Jackie was aptly named.
She had an uphill battle
hanging tough with me
before gettin' her ass free.

I didn't have my jones
to talk to on the phone,
but I was some long distance
motherfucker in my bones.

That's the thing with ex-addicts.
They act like goddamn butlers,
letting naked strangers
into their rented flesh.

THE MAN WITH THE HORN (1981)

Not one of your best discs.
Your chops down, you've abdicated
your throne, lost your slot as boss
of the baddest band in jazz. Stand
on the scorched earth of fusion,
Agharta and Pangaea behind you.

You dropped two bombs in Osaka
back in '75. Mtume, Foster,
Henderson setting the funk fuse,
Cosey and Lucas splitting atoms
on a twin-guitar attack, while
you and Sonny Fortune really blew.

You exposed the core, achieved
meltdown. Sat, bemused,
while all fusion's buildings lay flat.
Hip disintegrating, ankles aching,
ulcer acting up, in terrible pain,
you saw the sky burn an unearthly hue.

The sky bled, sun set. It didn't
rise for another six years and, still,
there were no pretenders to your throne.
The jazz landscape was full of holes.
You said you couldn't hear the music
after Osaka. You hung up your horn.

Now your embouchure and technique
are wanting. You settle for a calmer,
quieter muse. Call on your nephew,
younger players. Call in the favour
of Bill Evans on tenor and soprano.
Great funk/rock bass and guitar players.

They buoy you up while you wail
your mournful ballad sound through
simple rhythms, simpler changes,
looking for a new way. It hurts to hear
you lose so much, but you're back
and you're gonna say it. You're gonna say it.

"The Man With The Horn" is some
sad way of invoking the muse —
a pop praise song to the
better part of you. The player
in absentia. Not nearly the blues.
But "Aida" cooks with acetylene.

You wail after the bitch who
used to be your muse,
and we can't deride you,
for your cry is still there;
you tear the faded curtain
with such joyful riffs.
This new muse is still hip.

She's gonna be good to you. Her
honey flows into your horn, serves
notice that your "Back Seat Betty"
is not just some blonde with big tits.
She's calling from the far side of loneliness.

Somewhere east of Eden, west of Elysium
the lambs cavort and gambol. The notes
come frolicking home. More star people
are woodshedding. You can feel it
like sap running in the trees. The muse
is whispering, is whispering on the breeze.

THE KIX INCIDENT

The spring of '81. I'm really back,
ready to play in public again.
Freddy Taylor, a promoter in Boston,
books us into a club called KIX.

It's in the Cambridge area: uptown, hip.
Four days at the end of June
before we play George Wein's
Newport gig. We're in the pink.

I want everyone to know I'm back,
so I show up in my brand new
canary-yellow Ferrari coupe.
(A little show biz don't hurt sometimes.)

When I arrive there is a long line,
but a lot of folks are just waiting
to see if I'll show. When I do,
the line snakes around the block.

My band's pure nitro, total TNT:
Marcus Miller, Bill Evans, Mike Stern,
Al Foster, and Mino Cinelu. Capped
and primed. We blow everyone away.

Man, people were crying when they saw me,
crying when I played. It was amazing!
One night a little crippled black guy
parks his wheelchair in front of the stage.

I'm playing the blues and I know
this guy's gotta know some blues, so I
play my solo to him, catch his eye.
He's shakin', cryin' like a day-old baby.

Then he reaches up and touches my horn
like he was blessin' it — blessin' me.
I damn near lost it. Damn near broke
into tears myself. This cat was so beautiful.

I played like I'd never been away that night.
Played me some blues. Up, down, and sideways.
Marcus laid down such fat bass lines
and Al kept such a tight groove, I was floating.

The guys at Columbia got it all down
cos they thought I wasn't long for this world,
wanted to cash in on every blessed groove.
But, man, I was back; I was all the way home.

STAR PEOPLE

PARANOID

One time I'm driving my Ferrari
up West End Ave. Spot two cops
parked at the curb. They hail me —
all the cops knew me back then.
No big deal. We engage in small talk.

But two blocks later I look down
and in this compartment on the door
see this white powder and freak.
I never took coke out of my house,
so I think someone's planted the stuff.

I stop and abandon ship,
leave the Ferrari and keys
in the middle of the damn street!
I run into a building. No doorman.
Take the elevator to the seventh floor.

I hide in the trash room a long time
before I get a grip, come to my senses.
Luckily, no one has stolen my car.
The keys are still in it. Sky is grey,
white flakes tumbling pure cocaine.

"MILES AHEAD: A TRIBUTE TO AN AMERICAN LEGEND"
(Radio City Music Hall, November 1983)

Why is the audience so angry with me?
Why do they think I'm arrogant
because I cannot make a speech?
I spoke to them so eloquently just now.
I practically bled through my horn.
Every note said, "Thank you! Thank you!"
I'm crying inside, Can't they hear me?
Why do I need words to translate this feeling?
I'm grateful, you bastards, I'm grateful!

HONDA COMMERCIAL

One car commercial got me
more recognition and exposure
than all my years on stage
or layin' down bad tracks on wax.

After I did that Honda gig,
black and white, Puerto Rican,
Asian kids, kids I don't know
would stop me in the street.

"I know who you are!" they'd say.
"You're Mr. Tyson.
You're married to Cicely Tyson,
the great black American actress."

They were sincere, enthusiastic too.
That's what being a bad actor
on the great American boob tube
will do for you. I'm the Honda guy.

I live in the home of the brave,
drive an upholstered roller skate.
Hey, I'll do my hair in corn rows,
if you let me show you how to shave.

ONCE MORE, FOR GIL

I was talking to Gil
the week after he died.
I said, "Gil, why the fuck
did you die like you did?
Why did you go to Mexico
to make your final exit?"

Gil said, "I'm sorry, Miles,
but I had to go to Mexico.
It's the only way I could go.
I was never one for crescendos
or overwrought emotions. Sorry,
but I thought a fade-out was best."

I understood him because we
think alike and always have.
"Miles," he intoned, "play me
one of your muted solos?
Do 'Saeta' one more time —
just to say goodbye? I'd like that."

"You know you're in my bones, Gil,"
I replied. "You're inside me now.
I'll play fewer notes, more softly."
He said, "Play past what you know,
Miles, play past what you know.
We'll do 'Tosca' when you get here."

"When I get there, Gil, can we
look up Billie or Janis? Can we
do 'Summertime' one more time?
I liked the way you arranged Jimi's
unearthly blues. Can we maybe see
if he's learned to read music yet?

"I still have those charts I showed him
and Pete Cosey's fine, but — well —
I always wanted to play with Jimi.
We could re-invent acid funk.
Wouldn't that be a gas? I could
float our sound over his cry.

"We could do some real cerulean
preternatural blues, couldn't we?
I miss you, Gil. I don't know
if I told you, but you understood me
better than anyone. Better than I
understand myself these days.

"You were my best friend, Gil.
I love you, man. I know we'll
show the angels a thing or two
about cloud ten. It'll be better
than we ever were together here.
We'll really re-tune the spheres."

"Go easy, Miles. You know I was never
prolific, never was very organized.
I take a long time to do anything —
even here. But listen, man, it's OK.
Bird, Fat Girl, Trane are all here.
We'll make some fine music again."

So now I know, you know?
Gil's OK. He's not in any pain
and he's got a lot of hep cats
to play with. He's probably gone
electric. Probably already has a score
for Hendrix's guitar, my muted horn.

I don't worry about dying, even if I
have to fill Wallace Roney's ear
with everything I know. He's a great player.
And while Quincy is no Gil Evans,
he's been at me a while, you know.
So here we are at Montreaux again.

My chops aren't so good. I can't
get all those runs Gil and I did.
I haven't got the strength or wind.
Wallace is pinch-hitting though;
he'll do the high register stuff.
"They love us though, Gil, they really do."

FORGIVE ME, MY DEARS

Forgive me, my dears.
I loved you all; I loved you madly.
Forgive my wanderlust; forgive my anger.
Forgive my callousness; forgive my trysts.
I loved you all; I loved you badly.

I was only sixteen, sweet Irene.
You were only three years older.
What did I know of romantic love
that could make me your foot soldier?
Forgive me, love, I grew far too much older.

Forgive me, Cheryl, dearest.
I was but a child myself
when you graced our blank sheets.
Irene wanted a home, stability;
I had only white sheets to fill.

Forgive me, Gregory and Miles IV,
you came along when I was poor.
Poorest in love, saddled with domesticity.
I had a love in Paris
and, like Peter, couldn't keep her.

Forgive me Juliette of the Spirits.
We had no language but touch
and touching you was something
I could never get enough of.
I took to cranking you.

I didn't get to the bottom
of that dime bag for years.
A cliché, I know, but I
was beyond any white
crystalline veil you could find.

Forgive me, all you women
whose virtue was easier to attain
than any I lay claim to.
Forgive me for living off
the avails of your sloughed skins.

Forgive me, my honey brown dancer.
I loved you, Frances. I will rue
screwing up my chance with you
until the day I die. You are my
tone, the fecund earth from which I grow.

Forgive me, Cicely, I didn't
desire your body with the kind
of passion you kindled in my mind.
You were insistent and persistent though.
I should have let you go.

Instead, I beat down all your walls,
made myself an insensate ingrate
paranoiac paramour. I snorted so much snow,
talked more to my demons
than I talked to you.

Forgive me, Betty, You were twenty-three,
took me to Sly and Jimi,
updated my wardrobe.
I had no right to treat you
like the clothes I wore.

Forgive me, Marguerite,
for saddling you with my fourth child
while I snuck out in brothel creepers.
You stuck me out four years too long.

Forgive me, Erin, for doing that to you.
You, of all people,
my youngest child,
deserved a better father.
I had been around a block or three.

I should have tied a knot in my dick
instead of feeding it
down so many holes
like a garden hose.
What could I have flushed out?

And why do I speak of my dick
like it is some ebony trumpet?
It is only the tag end of me
I use to inflate
my terrible ego.

Forgive me, my dears.
I only ever wanted to hear
the music of the spheres.
Instead, I toyed
with taking you apart.

I have an unforgivable desire
to get inside a woman's skin.
I'm thick with skins myself —
an onion with no centre.

Forgive me if I abrade each layer
of the world in which I live.
I have only one blossom —
the flared bell of a trumpet
from which to leave a scent.

There is a piquancy,
a fragrance I cannot resist
that creates an aura
about the nape of all things
I long to nuzzle next to.

Forgive me, mother
for accusing you
of making my brother queer.
It's your lovely pearl-adorned ear
I could never whisper in enough.

STAR PEOPLE (1982)

For six years you
didn't touch your horn,
Then came the desultory playing
on The Man With the Horn,
the kick-ass warm-up gig
and Grammy for We Want Miles.

Now this long blues jam
to tell us you're back,
looking forward
to re-claiming your throne.

It's almost as if you were
asking politely for someone
to fill you in on what you
missed. Each note's a question.

But who are the Star People?
The little green men
who came out of the radiator?
Silhouettes out on the snow barrens?

The picayunish Miro pixies
who danced through your fingers
out of wax, into paint?

Blue meanies screaming
in your cranium for fast relief?
What is it they would say to you
of infamy or fame?

Do they beam you up
to some mother ship, or ship you
down the river in twofer offers
from the corporate vault when
you are noshing at Poor Yorick's?

Right now your painting and doodles
grace album covers and gallery walls.
John Scofield's guitar is scorching
a path that will leave no blade of grass.

Your timid horn goes hickory dickory
and there is this matter of the clock.
Miro and Basquiat
can't paint you out of this one.

MAD AT MILES

So now I'm the subject
of some feminist diatribe . . .
Wonderful! Some hard luck mama
wants all you sexy women
to boycott my concerts,
burn my records until I'm
straight on the women question.

Great! What women question?
I'm supposed to be some sexist prick
because I've admitted in print
I slapped Cicely silly one time
or call my women bitches?
Because I've got a salty tongue
and say a lot of dumbass things?

Man! That's such bullshit!
I love women! I love everything
about them: the way they walk,
the way they talk, the way they dress . . .
If I had a nickel for every bitch
that rode my horn, I wouldn't
need to play one, would I?

You don't think women come on to me?
I'm just using my little boy looks,
my wealth and fame to lay pipe —
like the friggin' Waterworks Department?
Gimme a break! I didn't invent the road!
I didn't buy into society's monogamous program!
You just want this nigger on a leash!

You think because I create beautiful music
I gotta be this button-down, skinny tie,
ivy league cat in black sunglasses:
a jazz spade who snaps his fingers
and doesn't wig when you replace the beret
with whatever other lid contains that cool,
existential thing. That's it, isn't it?

You want me to be your live evil prince,
your badass junkie pimp who
doesn't give a shit. A monkey in a suit
who'll jig for change to the tune
of your mad hurdy gurdy machine.
Well, fuck that! I like to fuck —
so do the women who play my horn.

I've never been no kind of husband, true.
I've done a lot of things I shouldn't have —
including hitting Cicely. But I don't hate
women. I don't use their bodies to
butt out my smoldering cigarette dick.
I love the women I'm with, and they love me.
It's real as long as it lasts. I'm real.

So what if my dream muse is some
Nefertiti in a bar who looks like Ma,
and I'm playing ring toss with
the blue smoke circles of my Galois
personality. I've made no secret of the fact
that this trumpet is my Lucille. She's sturdy.
She'll see me through the third act graciously.

TUTU (1986)

Some might call it funky late-night:
the synthesizer programming, percussion,
bass, drums, and other instrument tracks
having been pre-recorded, mixed down
before you ever got near the studio.

Some might point to Marcus Miller's
genius and studio wizardry, say
this is more his album than yours.
But then your presence, like Bishop Tutu's
at a political rally, galvanizes everything.

It's really the black magus, chairman Miles,
the funky emissary that floats his sound
down from the clouds to be with us here,
that ethereal Harmon mute and B-flat Martin
processed slick as unkinky hair that does it.

You insinuate yourself into the mix like
some electric honey bee in clover, each
haunting note probing for nectar,
picking up pollen from head to foot
and buzzing all up in our bodies. Pure mead.

Does the shadowman know more of joy
than he lets on? The wry nod to Nelson
Mandala and pun on your earlier "Half-
Nelson" hold on bop in "Full Nelson" here
is about wrestling with angels, walking on egg shells.

You take us to some funky stream if it isn't
the River Jordan. It's not the cross on
the noggin you're trying to give us
either, that's clear. But here's
one honky cat ready for the dunking.

Your music is a bath of fire and ash
if it isn't water and you are some
blue funk angel sanctified dipped and fried!
Cool and funky — that's a hip stunt, Miles.
Take the podium, chairman, blow Azania home!

AMANDLA (1989)

Zulu cry for freedom —
freedom from apartheid,
freedom from pain and want,
freedom from desire, the ravening cry
of your hungry horn. Freedom from
appetites, derision, scorn.

This your last studio recording
with members of a working band,
you take a stand,
go one better than your Tutu disc
now that you've gained ground
on your own lengthening shadow.

You keep the jackals at bay,
but sometimes when you seek poetry
you find pottery instead:
something like Keats's vase —
a serviceable container,
all of a piece —
without the infernal
posturing Greeks.

JACO PASTORIUS

Of Jaco what is there to say?
That he was a mother on electric bass?
That he played it like a lead guitar?

He was a drug-crazed egomaniac too.
Did some wicked slappin' and bowin'
on the bones of his jones, didn't get far.

"I'm Jaco fucking Pastorius," he crowed,
and cranked the volume so damn loud
the input and output channels both had to go.

Drug deal gone wrong? Money owed?
"I'm Jaco fucking Pastorius," he cried.
Someone beat him. The mother died.

LISTEN UP, WALLACE

Listen up, Wallace. I know
there ain't no way I can
tell anyone everything I know.

You got the cry, you got the tone.
You ain't no boney maroney
with jesus jumpin' in your bones.

You got no jones, no debt to me
for the chops I loaned.
Your muse be mannin' the phone.

Just take the calls. Listen
more than you talk. Talk
less than you play. You'll be OK.

The crickets will saw away
at the same spot on their legs,
intone their great profundo notes

about Montreaux, your stepping
into my shoes and shadow.
You'll have to go your way.

Improvise your life above
expectation and white noise.
Keep your dignity and poise.

You may have my tone,
avoid vibrato in plumbing
my cool, but you ain't no fool.

So fuck what the mothers say.
There ain't no cricket born
who can take that fact away.

A whole plague of locusts
might descend on the fields
you seed. You can't stop them

or predict the winds of change,
but you reap what you sow
outside the perimeter of stage

or studio. Trust me. I know.
Wallace Roney's gonna be a name
they want to lay claim to too.

Don't think the sun rises
between the cheeks of your ass,
and don't play in the shade.

Let 'em plant a flag in the soft
flesh of someone else's ass.
Use yours to pull out nails.

DOO BOP (1991)

They trashed you before;
they'll trash you again,
but what do they know,
these critics with haloes
that fit like turtlenecks
under bad herringbone?

Sure, you're only floating
muted cool/bebop phrases
over Easy Mo Bee's
hip hop dance tracks
while he and his studio
cronies rap bad lyrics,

but what of it? It ain't
jazz, it ain't abstract,
complicated. You ain't
playin' modal improvs
off the bass vamps, ain't
in no button-down groove.

And, yeah, two of the tracks
were cobbled together
from your unreleased
RubberBand session solos
and Easy's overdubs,
but what of that too?

You need a PhD
in kinesthetic and
post-bop harmelodics
to get down to a little
street jive? Cos that's
what it is. What he sez.

What it is don't need
no grammar to rhyme
or keep body time. What
it is is feel good riffs
for street kids who maybe
never heard of Easy or Miles.

What it is is infectious
rhythm, Jim, not no
Jim Crow Third Stream fantasy,
but Chocolate Chip Duke Booty:
a confection you put to the lip
so your feets get hip.

Miles heard the street sounds;
he heard sweet sounds
from a Manhattan brownstone;
heard 'em all up in his body
with hip hop. God playin' scratches
on an old platter moon.

He swayed beneath a street lamp
and made music their jones
to monkefy the mast. To get past
the jazz record stations and down
on the pavement. To get down.
To just blow. To get down and go.

He laid down six funky tracks,
six simple tunes to fuse
bebop to hip hop. Created
doo bop and went for
"a quick tune-up" in hospital.
Got down so far he dropped.

PANGAEA (1975)

GONDWANA

A new dawn. The first day amphibians
set foot on the steaming mud of creation,
a daunting bass vamp calls like something creeping
but the flute sings of treetops,
the promise of unsinged wings.

The calm after a storm perhaps,
this side of the disc a return to some strange
homeland of the senses — after the civil war
has rendered Rhodesia's colonialist past
into the promise of a Zimbabwe — and before
the internal growing pains would atomize all trust again.

The flute cries out this pain: the pain of accommodation,
re-evaluation and dances, dances over the beat,
trilling out your first horn solo
and your wah wah trumpet cries like a baby
softly, hesitantly, then begins to burble,
test new wings on the clear bright air.
And the sky is defiantly azure today,
the clouds thinned out to cirrus wisps
so the notes roll porpoise-like through the waves
and cavort and play around the edges
of a new melody. A simple blues tune this —
atmospheric and ethereal, but grounded too,
guitar trailing you like a dog at heel,
then going off to sniff the roses while the percussion
like new fronds unfurling dance in zephyrs
about fragments of the melody.

Then the drums and simple bass vamps
invite a re-grouping of the troops
and you come in with a tentative wah wah question:

What? What? Who when where why?
Now now now now now
and the guitar begins formulating its philosophy
and there is a general larruping and hubbub
on the land and your organ — sounding way off
in the distance like some gospel hymn
inviting the four-centuries old shredded wail
of wah wah blues from the lead guitar
Now a simple strut, now a deep mournful cry
of continents set adrift on the magma pool
of clustering, re-forming figures, notes, dreams, hopes.

Oh, you wanted Hendrix but couldn't get him —
and all because he was too embarrassed
to admit he couldn't read the scores
you'd left him before he de-camped for England
and choked on his own vomit. Yet found
something of him on the other side of the world
in these young turks you'd try first live,
improvising to the magma of unseen unheard blues
that might well have been a homage to him
and had them break through that hard crust
of effrontery, that salty ego act of yours
to express themselves within the taunting come-hither
of your unabashed cool sound and simmered
them down deep into a dark fathomless pool
of wah wah trumpet blues, soft, soft, so soft,
stepping, strutting out its quiet perambulations
inviting the second Benson-like guitar noodlings
into the groove. All the while one-hand vamping
organ chords long and thin as clouds drifting apart.

But wait! Wait! There is some new creature
calling its name from the canopy beneath the mist
and the bass wah wah speaks of a whole pond
of amphibious animals just now trying new limbs
on the land. The whole swamp is vamping its
larrup of joy and the guitar shreds
long thin notes like chromosomes lining up
to perform meiosis yet again.

And a wild electronic wind is brewing
catching at the leaves of trees until the
whole jungle is alive with shimmering
rain-spattered notes and a high long
strange whistle takes us out to the stratosphere.